Contents

Area Map Showing the Locations of the Walks

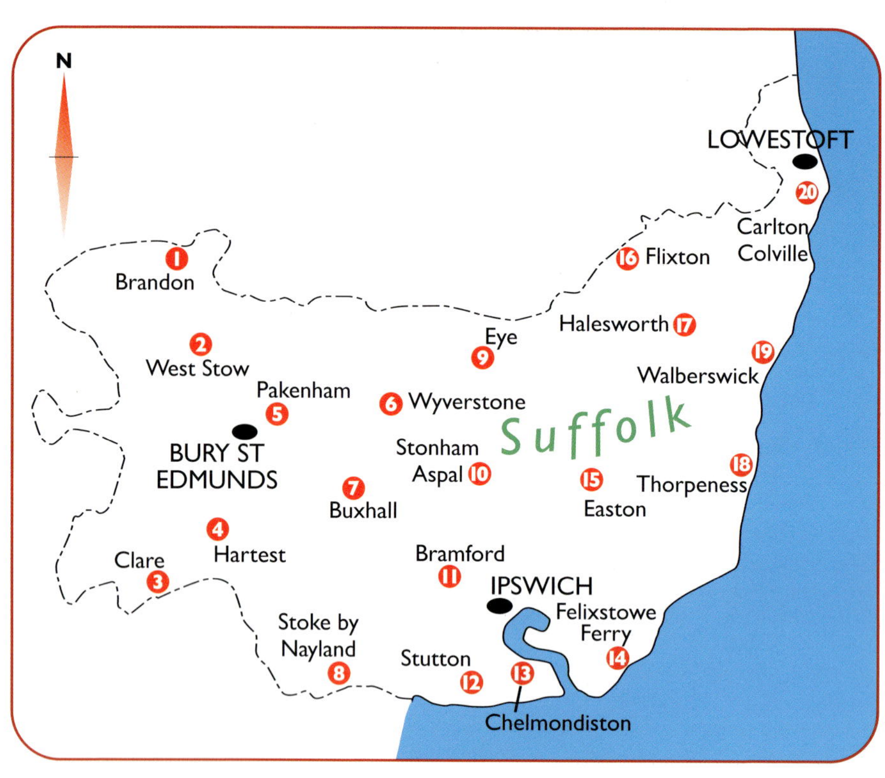

Kiddiwalks

IN
SUFFOLK

Laurie Page

COUNTRYSIDE BOOKS
NEWBURY BERKSHIRE

COUNTRYSIDE BOOKS
3 Catherine Road
Newbury, Berkshire

To view our complete range of books,
please visit us at
www.countrysidebooks.co.uk

ISBN 978 1 84674 190 6

Photographs by the author
Maps by CJWT Solutions

Designed by Peter Davies, Nautilus Design
Produced through MRM Associates Ltd., Reading
Typeset by CJWT Solutions, St Helens
Printed in Thailand

Contents

PUBLISHER'S NOTE

We hope that you obtain considerable enjoyment from this book; great care has been taken in its preparation. Although at the time of publication all routes followed public rights of way or permitted paths, diversion orders can be made and permissions withdrawn.

We cannot, of course, be held responsible for such diversion orders and any inaccuracies in the text which result from these or any other changes to the routes, nor any damage which might result from walkers trespassing on private property. We are anxious though that all details covering the walks are kept up to date and would therefore welcome information from readers which would be relevant to future editions.

The simple sketch maps that accompany the walks in this book are based on notes made by the author whilst checking out the routes on the ground. They are designed to show you how to reach the start, to point out the main features of the overall circuit and they contain a progression of numbers that relate to the paragraphs of the text.

However, for the benefit of a proper map, we do recommend that you purchase the relevant Ordnance Survey sheet covering your walk. The Ordnance Survey maps are widely available, especially through booksellers and local newsagents.

Introduction

What a beautiful county Suffolk is! There are some wonderful little villages and spectacular countryside scenery, as well as an interesting coastline that is very popular with the local people. I was delighted when I embarked on this Kiddiwalks project and have thoroughly enjoyed devising routes with children in mind.

Some fascinating places of historic interest are included and, in particular, locations that feature some of the county's best windmills. You will also find a route based on the splendid working watermill at Pakenham. A good walk for children must not be too long and should have interesting things to see and activities to keep them busy along the way. For the older ones, walking is a chance to educate them and foster an interest in nature. This book hopes to achieve that with routes featuring English trees, wild flowers and hopefully the opportunity to spot some of Suffolk's diverse wildlife. For younger children, feeding the ducks, spotting rabbits and squirrels and running free in the open air are perhaps preferable options.

Some places that I already knew well, among them Easton, Walberswick and West Stow, I was sure would appeal to children. But, of course, I also discovered some new locations that would fit in nicely with the publication: Clare was somewhere I had always meant to visit and it proved to be a real treasure; Stoke by Nayland is very quaint and the attractive River Blyth at Halesworth, with all its bridges, was a pleasant surprise.

All the walks are circular and are less than 4 miles – the longest, starting from the visitor centre to the south of Alton Water, is 3¾ miles. Where possible I have tried to stick to footpaths, bridleways and byways. On some routes I have included pavements, permissive paths and occasionally roads, but always with their suitability for family walks in mind. Where a circuit, or part of it, could be undertaken by pushchairs, I have mentioned it.

As a guide, I have allowed 30 minutes to cover a mile, assuming the youngsters to walk about 2 miles per hour. However, this is walking time only and does not incorporate any stops along the way, so if you are pausing to eat, viewing anything of interest or just resting, this has to be taken into account and the entire journey will probably take considerably longer – but that's half the fun!

In the rucksack parents should pack maps, cagoules in case of a shower, snacks and drinks for the younger members of the party, a camera, pens and sketch pads and plastic bags to collect wild fruit, leaves and anything else that takes the children's fancy. Binoculars are always useful, too.

Equipped with this book, parents and grandparents can keep the children occupied for hours, educate them along the way, and provide some wonderful memories of walks in the pretty villages and countryside of Suffolk.

Laurie Page

Brandon

Forest Paths Galore!

Brandon lies on the edge of Thetford Forest, close to the Norfolk border. Where there was once a country estate, a country park has been created with plenty of paths to explore. This circuit is short but manages to include most of the important features of the park, including the walled garden, a well, the lake, sculptures and the children's playground – in fact, something for everyone!

 **Getting there** *The entrance to Brandon Country Park can be found less than ½ mile south of Brandon, on the B1106. Approaching from the town, look for the sign to the park on the right.*

Length of walk 1¾ miles.
Time 50 minutes.
Terrain Easy, wide paths, suitable for pushchairs.
Start/Parking In the free car park next to the visitor centre at the park (GR 785853).
Map OS Explorer 229 Thetford Forest in The Brecks.
Refreshments The visitor centre has a tearoom called the Copper Beech, open throughout the year.

1 Go past the visitor centre at the end of the car park and follow

The Walk

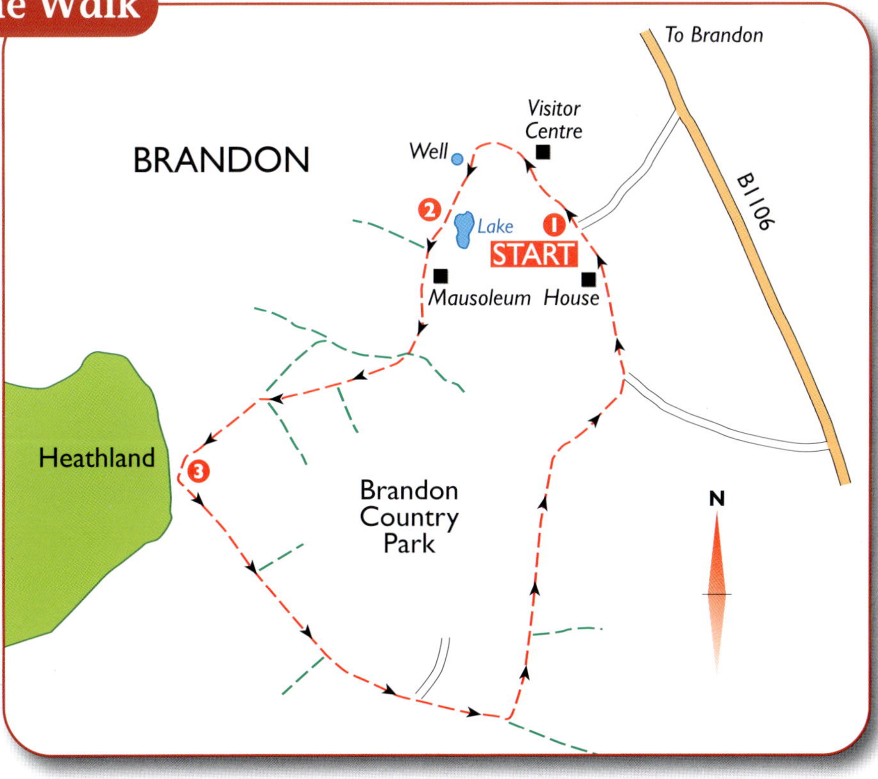

the sign to the Walled Garden. Take time to visit the garden and its well. As you leave the entrance to the garden turn right and then right again soon after at the next path junction. Keep to the main track, which emerges at a picnic area by the lake. Turn right (after taking a look at the information board) past the red safety ring. The path bends left by a seat to the next junction where there is an open view of the lake.

2 Turn right and follow the path, which goes gently downhill to some modern wooden sculptures and then swings left along a route through the trees. You will pass a mausoleum on the left; there is another information board here. At the next path junction turn right, following the sign to Brandon Park Heath. Almost at the end there is a path branching off to the left – but before you take this, go to the metal gate at the end and look for the sheep that graze on the heath and read the next information board. Return to the (now right-hand) path, which then swings left by a wire fence and continues through the trees.

◆ Fun Things to See and Do ◆

The **visitor centre** has some interesting activities. Children can engage in Stone Age pencil rubbings and use the scary touch and feel habitat experience. There is an interactive sound board and information on the history of Brandon and all about flint. If children would like to engage in organised pond dipping this can be arranged with the Park Ranger for a small charge (telephone: 01842 810185).

Here are **some questions** for the children. The answers are all to be found in the visitor centre:
1. How deep is the well?
2. On the walk, you pass a modern wood sculpture made by Keith Rand in 2006. What wood is it made from?
3. What famous Celtic Queen had her homeland here 2,000 years ago?
4. What type of sheep graze on the heathlands?

3 At the next junction by the blue post, turn left, going straight uphill. Observe the flint that lies on the path and around. At the top, by the cycle route information board, turn left and proceed down to the next junction where you turn sharp right, going back uphill. At the top, go round the metal gate and turn left past Brandon House along a hard park road. As the path swings right, go left into the parking area and the children's play area. Proceed on down, returning to the visitor centre.

◆ Background Notes ◆

In 1820 a successful businessman, **Edward Bliss**, bought a huge area of heathland, part of what is known as 'the Brecks'. He built a house there and planted thousands of trees. A walled garden with a well was added so that food could be produced to supply the house. The **mausoleum** was constructed because Edward Bliss wanted to be buried on his own estate. Sadly, his body was moved to the parish church when new owners took over the park.

The park had fallen into neglect by the end of the Great War and it is now managed by Suffolk County Council who converted it into **the country park** we see today and re-created some of the heathland. Brandon House itself is a private residential nursing home.

Flint can be found all around this part of Suffolk and, not far from here, about 4 miles away over the county boundary into Norfolk, there is Grimes Graves, a well known ancient flint mine. Flint was used by prehistoric farmers to produce tools for farming the land and weapons in order to hunt for animals. Later, flints were used to ignite guns and also to build walls and houses. The mausoleum is a good example of where flint has been used in a building.

Answers to the visitor centre quiz:
1. 23 metres   2. Oak   3. Boudica   4. Jacob's sheep

West Stow

In the Steps of the Invaders

A mile from the village of West Stow, a country park has been created on the edge of Thetford Forest. There are lakes, trees, a children's play area, a café and a visitor centre, which is the entrance to a re-created Anglo-Saxon village. This walk, which includes all the main features of the country park, first goes through woods containing tall, elegant Norwegian spruce trees and then follows an ancient byway that the Germanic invaders themselves will have known, before entering the park itself and continuing on a delightful path alongside the lake, with the River Lark running along on the other side.

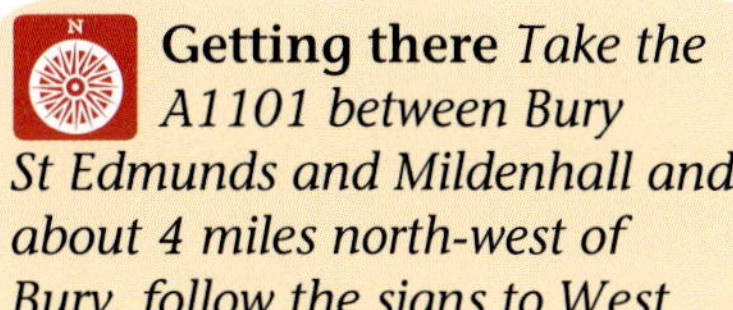

Getting there *Take the A1101 between Bury St Edmunds and Mildenhall and about 4 miles north-west of Bury, follow the signs to West Stow Country Park.*

Length of walk 2½ miles.
Time 1¼ hours.
Terrain The forest path at the beginning can be a little overgrown but there are no stiles and generally wide easy paths for the rest of the way, although the byway in point 2 may be rather muddy after heavy rain.
Start/Parking In the West Stow Country Park free car park (GR 802713).
Map OS Explorer 229 Thetford Forest in The Brecks.
Refreshments The café next to the visitor centre serves lunches and light snacks.

The Walk

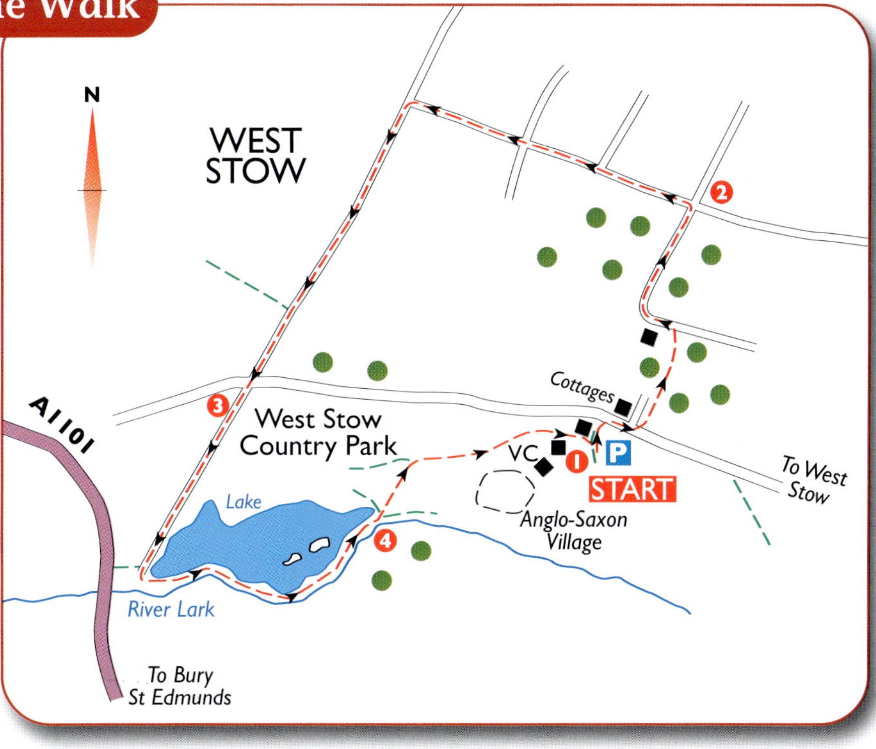

2

1 From the car park, go back to the road and turn right. Pass the pretty cottages and on the left, just the other side of the private track to Wideham Farm, take a narrow grass path that runs alongside the tall Norwegian spruce trees. This winding path goes through the ferns and underneath the low branches of an oak tree. It emerges onto a more distinct path. Turn left along this path, which bends right and goes gently uphill to a path crossroads junction.

2 Here you turn left again, along a wider dirt track that runs in a straight line for some distance. Go right to the end by the broken metal barrier and the T-junction with a byway. Turn left down the byway (this track is open to vehicles) and proceed down to the end where you meet the road. Cross over carefully (watching out for traffic) and take the track on the opposite side, going through the trees.

3 Pass the pedestrian entrance to the country park on the left. You will see the lake through the trees on the left. At the end of the track you emerge at a little parking area. Go through the gate on the left into the park. Turn right, taking the grass path

◆ Fun Things to See and Do ◆

There is a wildlife board in the café at the visitor centre that lists all the **animals** that live in or visit the park. See how many you can spot as you walk round. Just while we were drinking our coffee I was delighted to see a stoat appear by the bird table. And it wasn't on the list!

The children will enjoy getting rid of any surplus energy in the **playground**, which is located near the entrance to the park.

A visit to the **Anglo-Saxon village** is thoroughly recommended. It has been created so that it looks like a community residence that would have existed over a thousand years ago, including animal pens. Re-enactment days take place and provide amusement for all the family.

that runs around the lake. There are places to stop and view the lake and seats further on if you want to have a rest. The River Lark runs along on the right. Continue to the path junction by the wooden gate.

4 Here there is the option of three paths. Take the middle one, going past the wooden seat, over a ditch and on through another wooden gate. Continue straight on, through a further wooden gate. On the right can be seen the huts of the Anglo-Saxon village. The path follows the high wire fence and when it leaves this fence, you reach a path T-junction. Turn right back to the car park.

◆ Background Notes ◆

East Anglia was an area of England where the Saxons and the Angles permanently settled from the 5th century onwards. In 1965 there began an extensive excavation over several years to reveal the site of a large **Anglo-Saxon village** at West Stow. The artefacts and pottery found here helped to date it; occupation was from the early 5th century to the beginning of the 7th century. Dozens of small huts were built around large halls and the community farmed the local land, growing crops in the fields, with pigs, cattle, chickens, geese and goats kept as livestock. The River Lark close by kept the villagers supplied with fresh water and fish.

Several huts have been reconstructed and by way of experiment these huts have been built using different methods. There is a sunken hut, a raised hut and a hall with a fire in its centre. Between April and September, the village has visits from various historical groups, some in period dress. They exhibit the weapons used at the time, cook the type of food that was eaten, and demonstrate weaving and basket-making. The village is open all year round. For admission prices, times of opening and a calendar of special events, log on to www.stedmundsbury.gov.uk or telephone 01284 728718.

Clare

On the History Trail

The motte, with the remains of the stone keep

Although Clare is only small, there is much going on here. This ancient wool town contains Suffolk's oldest public country park and has a ruined castle to fire the children's imagination, an old priory and a fascinating little museum. Starting alongside the castle, the walk takes you towards the priory and alongside the River Stour before heading north past the common and circling down on the other side of the town, ending with a stretch alongside the former Stour Valley Railway line.

Getting there *Clare lies between Haverhill and Sudbury on the A1092. As you approach the centre of the town from Haverhill, turn right, following the sign that says 'Country Park' and 'Parking'.*

Length of walk 3¼ miles.
Time 1¾ hours.
Terrain There is very little road walking and good paths virtually all the way round so this route would be suitable for pushchairs though there is one stile to negotiate.

The Walk

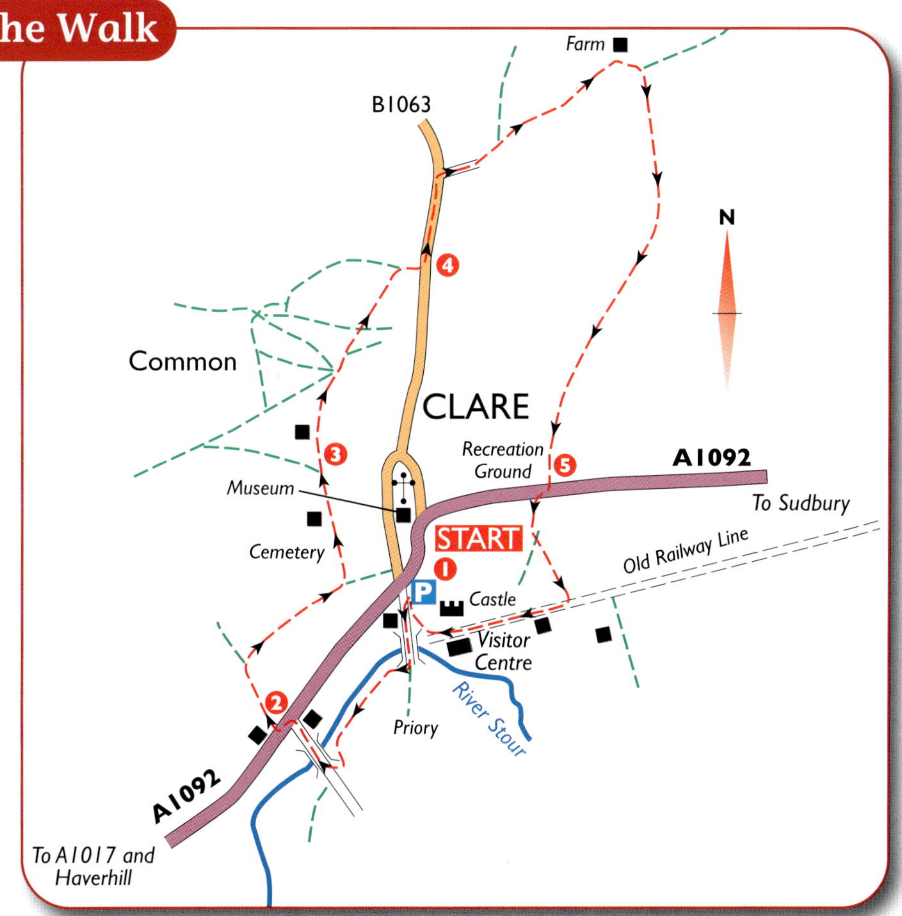

Kiddiwalks in Suffolk

Start/Parking In the pay and display car park at Clare Castle Country Park (GR 770453).
Map OS Explorer 210 Newmarket & Haverhill.
Refreshments There are four pubs in the town, all with gardens: the Bell, the Swan, the Cock and the Globe. There is also Café Clare in Well Lane and the antique shop at the start of the walk has a tearoom. Alternatively, you could picnic in the country park.

1 From the car park, go to the antique shop by the entrance and turn left towards Clare Priory. Go over the bridge and turn right (straight on and bear right to view the priory), following the pretty path that runs along by the river. When you reach the road, turn right over the blue bridge and proceed to the road junction. Turn left then immediately right up a footpath on the other side of the road.

2 Go uphill and at the first path junction turn right, heading towards the church. At the far corner of the field, turn left (straight on to visit the museum) and in the next corner of the field the path 'S' bends through a gap in the hedge. Continue on a hard path through the cemetery. Keep straight on at the red-brick building and straight on again at the next junction.

3 Cross the road by the school and pass through double wooden gates onto the common. At the junction of many paths, bear right to the right side of the mound. Keep to the path going

◆ Fun Things to See and Do ◆

The country park has an **adventure playground**, a **visitor centre** and places to **fly a kite** on a windy day and of course the castle ruins are there to explore.

The **little museum** by the church in the centre of the town is free to children under 16 and is open from Thursday to Sunday between April and September. See if anyone can spot the marmalade cutter, the leather fire bucket and a 17th-century treasure chest.

Clare museum

right, heading towards the cottages and houses. At the fork stay left. The path curves around the common, taking you to the other side where at another little junction you turn right, through the gap between the bank, leading to a stile. On the other side turn right to the road.

4 Turn left and use the walkway on the other side. Then turn right down the next road, called Hermitage Meadow. As the road bends, keep to the right along a concrete track. Cross the brook and continue along the drive past the house. The path swings right by the barns and goes through the hedge into a large field. Turn right along a wide field-edge path, which then diverts right into the trees. It meanders through the woods and emerges by a large shed. The now stony path converts to a tarmac path. Proceed past the recreation ground to reach the road.

5 Turn right and very soon go left down a footpath by the graveyard. At the 'Country Park'

sign go left at the fork and left onto a hard path. This goes through the trees with water on either side. At the next junction turn right, alongside the line of the disused railway. You will see the old station on the left and the motte and bailey castle to the right. Continue past the visitor centre back to the car park.

◆ Background Notes ◆

Clare Castle Country Park is set in 25 acres of woodland and grassland and the River Stour flows through the park. The **castle** is a typical Norman motte and bailey castle, constructed within 25 years of the Norman Conquest. It originally had a wooden tower on the top, which was replaced by a stone keep, the remains of which you see today. The castle was abandoned in the 15th century. The **visitor centre** near to the castle has displays about its history and lots of interesting information. Within its ramparts is the old **railway station**, opened in 1865. This was once a very busy place, transporting goods and passengers to London and the coast. It closed in 1967 but the old platforms and the station building remain. There is a **variety of wildlife** in the park including a flower called the Oxford ragwort but known as the railway flower because it seems to thrive along railway cuttings. There is also an **adventure play area**. The park is open all year round and holds special children's events from time to time. The visitor centre is open every day from April to September (telephone: 01787 277491).

Clare Priory is very old and was visited by friars in the 13th century. Although it was dissolved by Henry VIII, the 14th-century Friar's House, the cloisters and the Old Infirmary, which has been converted into a church, have survived. The Priory was re-established in 1953 and Augustinian Friars can once again be found living there.

The **Ancient House** next to the church of St Peter and St Paul in the town centre was built in 1473 and became the museum in 1979. Its plasterwork is very distinctive. The website www.ancient-house-museum.co.uk gives details of opening times.

Hartest

A Wild Flower Paradise

The Crown pub has an excellent play area for children

This walk displays the Suffolk countryside at its best. Hartest is a beautiful little village nestling in the hills. It has many characteristics of a typical old English community, with its parish church, ancient pub, the village sign on the green, and thatched cottages. An ideal summer outing, this short circuit provides the opportunity for children to appreciate and learn about wild flowers which are at their most prolific at this time of the year.

4

Getting there *Hartest lies on the B1066, which runs north to Bury St Edmunds. The village hall is opposite the village green by the crossroads.*

Length of walk 2 miles.
Time 1 hour.
Terrain A simple walk with no stiles. The area is quite hilly but the paths are good and the steepest gradient is downwards, near the end of the walk.
Start/Parking In the free car park by the village hall (GR 833525).

Map OS Explorer 211 Bury St Edmunds & Stowmarket.
Refreshments The Crown pub in the village has plenty of outside seating areas and a wonderful children's play area in the garden.

1 From the car park entrance, turn left to the road junction by the village green and go almost opposite, signposted to Chadacre and Shimpling. Proceed down the lane through the village, past the pub and the church and over the bridge to the road junction, where you turn left towards Lawshall

The Walk

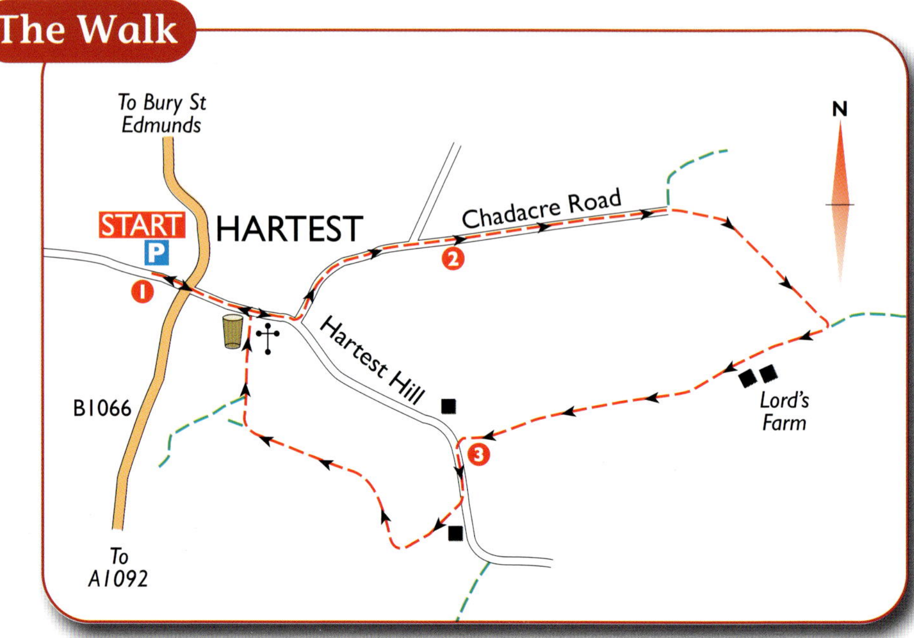

Hartest's delightful village green

and Cockfield. At the next junction go right uphill along the no through road.

2 This lane is full of wild flowers in season, along by the hedgerow. The main path converts to a stony track, then back to a concrete surface again. When you reach the junction at the top of

◆ Fun Things to See and Do ◆

Try and identify all the different **wild flowers** you find along the route. Taking a flower book with lots of pictures on the walk with you is a good idea. You shouldn't pick wild flowers but leave them for other people to enjoy. In any case there is little point in picking them as the majority will wilt and die long before you get them home.

And once the children have tired of looking for wild flowers, the village green in Hartest is an ideal spot to **fly a kite** if it is a windy day.

4

the hill, go right along the hard track. At the farm buildings bear right along a wide grass path with lovely views of the countryside to the right. You are then steered left to avoid the private path. Continue along what is a bridleway with more wild flowers and crop fields on either side. At the end of this path you come to a wooden gate by the road.

3 Turn left uphill. At the thatched Pippin Cottage, turn right along a grass footpath. This bends sharp right and then, after veering left, drops steeply downhill. The village can be seen in front. Before you reach the bottom, there is a footpath post on the right, taking you down a pretty path through the trees. Cross the bridge at the bottom and pass the pub on the left. You reach the road. Turn left and retrace your steps back to the junction and the car park.

◆ Background Notes ◆

The **wild flowers** that grow all around us in the summer are often taken for granted. But they provide an abundance of beauty and colour, the yellows, blues, pinks and white splashes amongst the green meadows and hedgerows, or an array of red poppies in a field. On this route in July, for example, there can be seen poppies, cow parsley, buttercups and more – we found 14 different species on our walk! Also watch out for the crops growing, particularly wheat, barley and peas.

The **Hartest Stone** is a huge limestone boulder that lies on the north end of the village green. There are a few stories relating how it got there but the one I like the best says that in 1713 it was dragged from Somerton on a sledge by 'twenty gentlemen and twenty farmers', to celebrate the Peace of Utrecht and Marlborough's victories in the War of the Spanish Succession. It is depicted on the village sign along with a stag or hart, which may also be where the village got its name.

The **Crown pub** in Hartest was a courthouse in the 16th century.

5

Pakenham

A Miller's Delight

Pakenham watermill

Suffolk has many mills – both windmills and watermills – around the county. It is rare these days to find a working mill, but Pakenham is unique in that it is the only village in England to have both a working watermill *and* a working windmill. Ideally you should plan to undertake the walk when the watermill is open, not only to see it in action, but also because it includes a permissive path along by the river, which is not accessible when the mill is closed. The alternative, slightly longer route is entirely on lanes, but both circuits give you good views of the two mills.

5

Getting there *From the A143 between Bury St Edmunds and Diss, turn off a few hundred yards south-east of the junction with the A1088 onto Mill Road. The watermill is a little way down on the right. There are brown mill signs to help you.*

Length of walk 2¼ miles (using the permissive path from the watermill) or 2¾ miles.

Time 1 hour and 10 minutes, with the longer route taking an extra ¼ hour.

Terrain Mostly road walking, unless you can incorporate the streamside path from the watermill. Luckily there is not much traffic on these lanes, so use the wide grass verges and be

The Walk

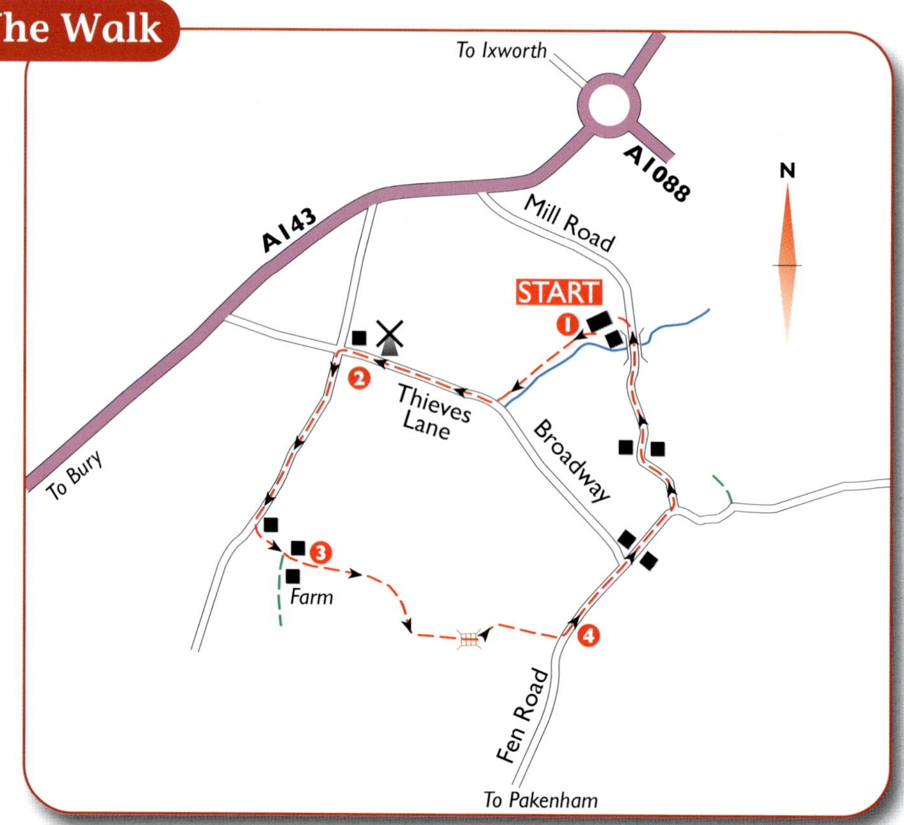

aware of approaching vehicles.
Start/Parking At Pakenham Watermill where there is free parking (GR 937695).
Map OS Explorer 211 Bury St Edmunds & Stowmarket.
Refreshments There is a tearoom in the Miller's House at the watermill, open at the same times as the mill. Pakenham has the Fox pub and there are two pubs in the High Street at Ixworth.

1 At the rear of the mill take the pretty 'Riverside Walk', which runs alongside the stream on a wide grass path. You will get a good view of the windmill from this path. Go to the end, where you will reach the lane. Turn right and go uphill. Before long the windmill comes into view again and you may wish to tarry awhile and look round before continuing on your way. Proceed to the road junction.

If you undertake this walk when the watermill is closed, you should continue down Mill Road (away from the A143) to the junction where you turn right along Fen Road and then soon after right into Broadway, which leads to Thieves Lane, joining the route above at the point where the waterside walk emerges onto the road (see map). This adds an extra ½ mile.

2 Turn left along the road. There is no pavement but you can use the raised grass verges on both sides. Proceed to Old Hall Farm, enjoying good views of the countryside as you walk, then take the footpath on the left along a tarmac service road, passing through the farm buildings and straight on down a wide grass path.

◆ Fun Things to See and Do ◆

Visit the watermill, if it is open, and find out about the life of a miller and how flour is made. The volunteer staff at the mill are very helpful and informative. They explain the whole process from start to finish.

For this walk **sketchbooks** are a good idea for older children. There are many things crying out to be drawn – including, of course, the watermill and the windmill.

5

3 At the metal gates follow the sign to the right, taking what may be a slightly overgrown path in places, running along a fence. At the end is a stile where you go left. Then go over a little bridge and turn left and then right along by a wire fence eventually leading to the stile by the lane.

4 Turn left by cottages and houses. At the road junction, go straight on. At the next junction, follow the watermill sign, staying on the road, which bends to the left. Pass more cottages and a rare old red telephone box. After another 200 yards you arrive back at the watermill.

◆ Background Notes ◆

The present **watermill at Pakenham** dates from about 1814 when it was restored but it stands on the foundations of a much earlier Tudor mill. On the first Thursday in the month, volunteers demonstrate the whole milling process and explain how the miller, from his position on the milling floor, produced the wholemeal flour. This is for sale at the watermill. A 17 horsepower oil engine made about 1904 was brought from another mill and installed at the Pakenham watermill in the 1930s. This replaced a steam engine and was used as auxiliary power in times of drought or when the pool was frozen. The engine is on display. The mill is open from April to November on Saturday and Sunday afternoons and Thursdays from 9 am to 4 pm. It also opens on bank holidays and there are special events during school holidays. There is a small admission fee. Full details are available on the website: www.pakenhamwatermill.co.uk or you could telephone 01359 232025.

The **Pakenham windmill** is a tower mill built of brick in 1831. It is 80 ft tall. The mill underwent restoration in 2000, partly funded by the Heritage Lottery Fund, and now the sails turn and flour is again ground in the mill, but these days electricity is used for this. You can go in and look round during working hours. Telephone: 01359 270570.

Wyverstone

Pond Life and Wild Berries

Wyverstone is a small village deep in the heart of the Suffolk countryside. There are no shops, only the parish church and lots of cottages, some thatched. The walk starts from the village hall in the centre of Wyverstone, located next to the children's play area. The route takes you over farmland and alongside laden hedgerows to the south and west, with a wonderful pond to enjoy two-thirds of the way round. At various places on the circuit, including Normans Farm and Fresh Winds cottage, seasonal fruit and vegetables are left for sale on a table out by the roadside or the front of the house.

Kiddiwalks in Suffolk

6

Getting there *The B1113 runs north from Stowmarket to Rickinghall. Turn off westwards into Bacton and when you reach the Bacton Bull pub, turn right to Wyverstone. At the T-junction in the village, you will see the village hall almost opposite.*

Terrain This is an easy, flat walk with very wide grass paths and a little lane walking.
Start/Parking The large free parking area at the village hall (GR 040678).
Map OS Explorer 211 Bury St Edmunds & Stowmarket.
Refreshments The thatched Bacton Bull, less than a mile away, has a large garden and a separate restaurant.

Length of walk 2½ miles.
Time 1¼ hours.

The Walk

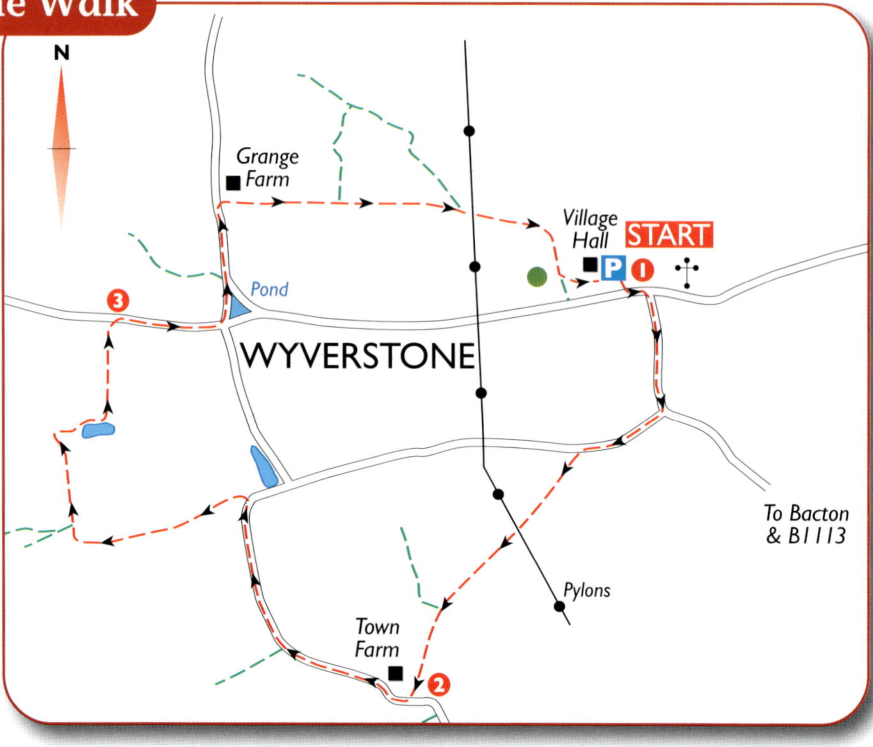

1 From the village hall car park, turn left along the road. At the next junction, turn right down Church Hill towards Bacton. At the next road junction at the bottom, just before the pink-coloured, thatched Normans Farm, turn right towards Earls Green. Just after the bend, take the footpath on the left, going across the field. Pass under the pylons to the footpath post by the hedgerow. Take the left path, which follows a little ditch to the right. This leads you to a lane.

2 Turn right and proceed along this quiet lane. Pass the pretty thatched Town Farm. Continue straight up for some distance to where the lane turns sharply to the right. On the crown of the bend, if you don't have a pushchair with you, take the unmarked footpath to the left, a wide grass path running alongside a large field. Eventually, the path turns 90° to the right. At the footpath post soon after, go straight on over the bridge and into the next field. This turns right again, rounds an overgrown pond and then turns left along a wide stony, double track which leads to the road. *(If you do have a pushchair, when you reach the crown of the bend, continue along the lane to the next*

◆ Fun Things to See and Do ◆

Youngsters will enjoy the opportunity to do some **pond dipping** at Crooksell Pond if they have a fishing net and a jam jar at the ready. Do remember that they should put everything back when they have finished and wash their hands at the first opportunity.

There is a **mini assault track** for children under 14 in the park next to the village hall.

In late summer, all the family can pick **blackberries** to add to apple pie and **damsons** to make jam, both to be found on the way round. It is a good idea to keep a plastic bag or container in your rucksack when you are walking, so that any fruit or other tasty morsels growing wild can be taken home.

junction and turn left which brings you directly to Crooksell Pond.)

3 Turn right into Wyverstone Street, heading towards the village. When you reach the road junction, Crooksell Pond can be seen on the corner and behind is Crooksell Hall. Turn left up Potash Lane. At Grange Farm turn right along a bridleway called Green Walk. Pass a bright blue house. Further on the path narrows through the trees. At the path junction by a seat, go straight on. The path then bends to the right and just before it terminates at the road, go through the gate on the left, over the children's play area and back to the village hall.

The village hall at the start of the walk

◆ Background Notes ◆

Crooksell Pond contains not only fish but also all sorts of pond life such as water boatmen and skaters, water beetles, water snails and sometimes newts.

It is free to pick fruit and berries from the outside of hedgerows – and this is called foraging – but if you want to enter fields then you must ask permission. The favourite foraging fruit is blackberries, available in the late summer and early autumn. Sloes and damsons make excellent jam. Elderflowers can be picked for home-made cordial and, later in the year, elderberries for wine. And in the fields and the woods various mushrooms can be gathered but be very careful that they are edible and you are not picking poisonous ones – an identification book would be useful.

Buxhall

A Hidden Gem

Although Buxhall is only a few miles from Stowmarket, it is a very quiet and scattered community featuring a church, a pub and an old converted windmill. This delightfully tranquil countryside walk, with some splendid scenery, is lovely at any time of year – but if you are there between Easter and October, you have the added bonus, halfway round, of a wonderful little museum depicting rural Suffolk life in the past and exhibiting some local arts and crafts.

7

Getting there *Turn westwards off the B1115 Stowmarket to Hadleigh road at Great Finborough and follow the sign to Buxhall.*

Length of walk 2½ miles.
Time 1¼ hours.
Terrain Good footpaths with some modest ups and downs but no stiles; very little road walking.
Start/Parking In the free car parking area in front of the parish church (GR 003576).

Map OS Explorer 211 Bury St Edmunds & Stowmarket.
Refreshments There is a small tearoom at Brook Farm, open at the same times as the museum. Buxhall Crown Inn is in Mill Road near the windmill.

1 Go through the gate leading to the church. At the porch entrance walk left round the church and through a wooden gate, then a metal one. Proceed up a hedge-lined grass path leading to a pretty thatched

The Walk

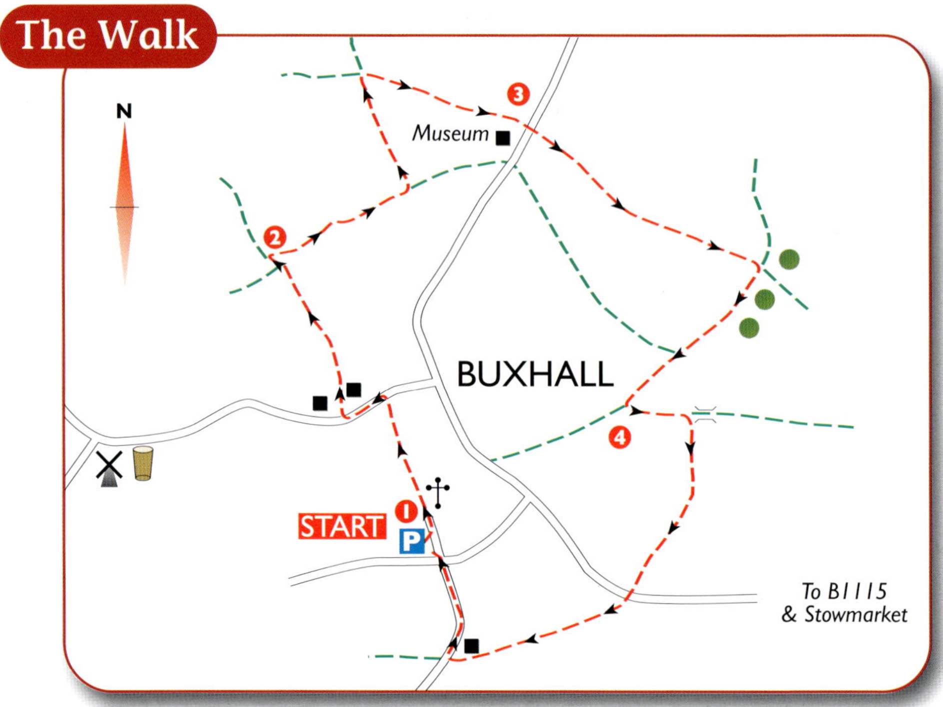

cottage by the lane. Turn left and then soon after take the footpath on the right the other side of the two pink thatched cottages. Go past the farm sheds and down a wide grass path. At the bottom go straight on, crossing the brook, and at the footpath junction, where there is a signpost, turn right.

2 Follow the path that runs parallel with the brook. At the little railway sleeper bridge, as you enter the next field, go left uphill alongside the field. At the top of this field, at the footpath crossroads, turn right, going under telegraph wires. To the right can be seen the church and further to the right the sail-less windmill. Continue to the caravan field and the farmhouse. Here is the little museum.

3 After leaving the farm museum, at the road take the footpath almost opposite up the steps. Go alongside the field. Further along there is a good view of the church in the neighbouring village of Great Finborough. The path descends to the end of the field. Do not go through into the wood but turn right, keeping the wood to your left. The path curves right. Go over a wooden bridge and head towards the telegraph pole but before you reach it you arrive at a footpath junction in the middle of the field.

◆ Fun Things to See and Do ◆

Visit the little **rural museum at Brook Farm**, which is free of charge. See if the children can work out what the toys were and how youngsters would keep themselves amused 100 years ago. They might like to find out the date of the Austin A30 and how much it cost to build the windmill in 1814.

Buxhall church acts as a landmark during the walk. See how many times the children can spot the church on the way round. Take a compass and the older children can work out the direction of the church from where they are on the walk.

4 Turn left. At the end of the field, turn right before the footbridge. Follow the stream for some distance. You eventually emerge at the road. Turn left over the road bridge and then immediately after take the footpath on the right. Keep the hedge and ditch to your right and at the end of the field by the cottage, bear right to the lane (Valley Lane). Turn right. The lane bends left and goes uphill back to the church.

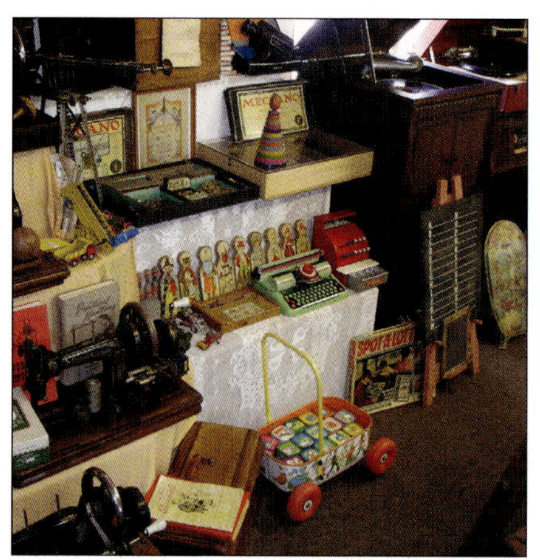

The museum has a wonderful display of

◆ Background Notes ◆

The **windmill**, which can be seen at the west end of the village, close to the pub, is now in private hands. It is a 19th-century tower mill with six floors and once had five millstones, more than average for a windmill. It eventually became an engine-driven mill right up until the 1970s. Unfortunately, it no longer has its sails. The original windmill at Buxhall was a post mill built around 1783 but it was made of wood and burnt down. It was suspected that the cause was arson.

The **Brook Farm museum** depicts Suffolk life over the last hundred years or so. The items on display include many facets of life in previous generations. The children will be interested in the toys, among them a Meccano construction set and a bagatelle table. You will also find some of the first televisions, gramophones, old sewing machines and typewriters and fascinating bygone kitchen equipment including a mangle and a butter churn. Some lovely old classic and vintage cars, which even the dads may not remember, are on display too. For opening times, telephone: 01449 736363.

NB: The Austin A30 is dated 1955 and the windmill cost £528 9s 1¼d.

Stoke by Nayland

And What's Your Name?

Cherry Tree Cottage – one of the many delightful homes in the village

Stoke by Nayland is a pretty village with some 'chocolate box' cottages, a splendid church, which has been painted by John Constable, and, opposite the church, a half-timbered guildhall dating from the 16th century and now converted into cottages. In times gone by, most houses in villages and in the countryside were not allocated numbers but were given names. As you go round, ask the youngsters to see how many cottages they can spot with their quaint names on display.

Starting in the village, the route takes you along part of the Stour Valley Path down towards the flat floodplains of the River Box and through farmland, passing the old mill and back up to the village again.

Kiddiwalks in Suffolk

8

Length of walk 2 miles.
Time 1 hour.
Terrain There are a couple of stiles to negotiate, as well as a little road walking.
Start/Parking In the free car park by the British Legion hut next to the recreation ground (GR 985363).
Map OS Explorer 196 Sudbury, Hadleigh & Dedham Vale.
Refreshments There are two pubs in the village centre, the Crown and the Angel Inn, both with outside areas and the Angel is particularly children-friendly.

1 From the parking area, turn left along the lane towards St Mary's church. At the church, follow the footpath sign on the left, going through the churchyard and past the main entrance to the church with its magnificent old carved wooden door. Continue to the main road. Turn left along the pavement and at the crossroads go straight over

◆ Fun Things to See and Do ◆

There are lots of **interesting cottages and houses** along the way, especially in Scotland Street. Many are pretty thatched cottages and some are timbered houses. See if the children can find the names of these dwellings and try to work out the reasons for them. Along the way they will see Half Moone, Tanglewood, Knutmill, Cherry Tree and The Old Bakehouse, but also many more. Older children could write them all down and decide which ones they like best. Everyone will enjoy joining in and choosing a name for a cottage of their own – something they saw along the route or one they thought up. The younger children can count the number of thatched cottages they pass during the journey. They can also see how many **farm animals** they can identify on the route.

"

The Walk

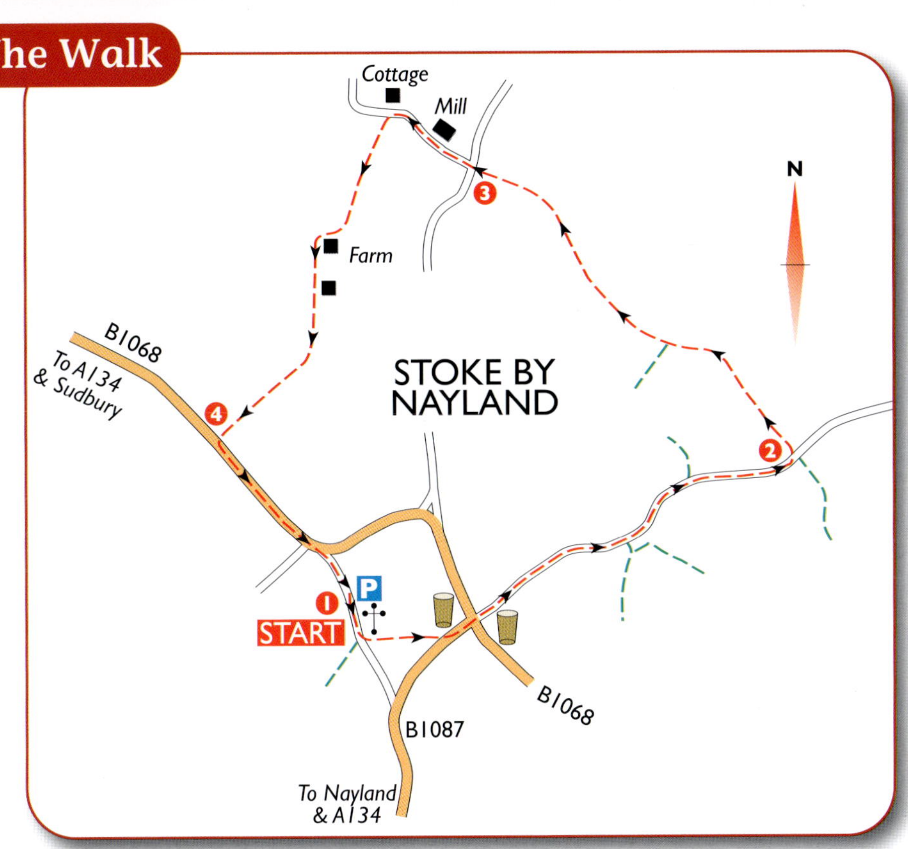

down the lane called Scotland Street. Proceed down the lane past many pretty thatched cottages. Ignore the first footpath on the left but continue downhill, enjoying the good view ahead. Before Scotland Place, opposite the beautifully converted black barn, take the footpath on the left.

2 This follows along the edge of a field. Bear right through the rusty gate and then follow the footpath sign through the right-hand metal gate of the two ahead and you will pass a variety of farm animals such as geese, chickens, pigs and sheep. Follow the farm track for some distance, passing through another metal gate and along a wide grass path. The church and water tower can be seen to the left. At the end of

8

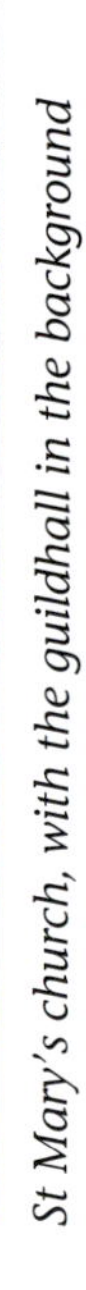

St Mary's church, with the guildhall in the background

the path, go over the stile next to the wooden gate by the road.

3 Continue along Mill Lane almost opposite, taking you past Polstead Mill. When you reach Maritime Cottage watch out for the footpath sign on the left, going alongside a hedge to your right. The route takes you gently uphill to a farmyard. Bear right around the back of the wooden sheds with a field to the right, then bear left across the brook into a meadow, keeping the hedge to your left. The path then veers left between large oaks, followed by a bend right going uphill with the grass footpath running parallel to a farm track. You will then reach the main road.

4 Turn left along the pavement. Continue straight on at the next junction and straight on again at White Horse Cottage, up School Street, so-called because this is where the 19th-century primary school stands, opposite your starting place.

◆ Background Notes ◆

Many **thatched cottages** can be seen in villages all over Suffolk. In Stoke by Nayland they are in abundance. Thatch is the traditional roofing material for houses and up to the early 19th century most homes were thatched. Wheat straw is the material that is used most and if done properly a thatched roof can last up to 50 years. Thatching is a trade that declined rapidly for many years but is now showing some rejuvenation, and it requires much craftsmanship. First the thatch is tied in bundles, then laid in an under-layer on the roof beams and pegged in place with rods made of hazel or withy. Then an upper layer is laid over the first, and a final reinforcing layer added along the ridgeline. Thatched properties are very attractive and the subject of many artists.

Half-timbered buildings, such as the old guildhall opposite the church, were popular during the Tudor period. The walls have a timber frame, usually beams of oak, a hard, tough wood, which is why the houses last so long. The areas between the frame were infilled with wattle-and-daub (upright branches interwoven by smaller branches and covered by a thick coat of clay mud), laths and plaster, or bricks. When bricks became abundant, half-timbered houses went out of fashion but today the blackened and warped timbers give these buildings an attractive 'olde worlde' look.

Old buildings and ancient monuments are protected by becoming **listed buildings**. Our most important historic buildings are Grade I listed and others are Grade II listed.

Guilds were ancient associations of craftsmen who would use the guildhall as their meeting place.

9

Eye

A Feast of Trees

A view of Eye from the castle site

Eye is a quaint old market town close to the Norfolk border and it has many historical features to enjoy after the walk, including fragments of the Norman castle. Starting from the nature reserve alongside the River Dove, this lovely route circumnavigates the town; much of it is in the rural suburbs where you wander across fields and farmland, through woods and along lanes where there is a wealth of native deciduous trees to admire. The children will enjoy trying to identify the trees by their leaves and shape.

Getting there *Eye lies a few miles east of the A140 to the south of Diss. From the town centre, travel east on the B1117 and after the church take the first road on the right, Ludgate Causeway.*

Length of walk 3½ miles.
Time 1¾ hours.
Terrain There are a few stiles to negotiate and a few roads to cross but the majority of the walk is along good footpaths.
Start/Parking In the free car park at the Pennings

The Walk

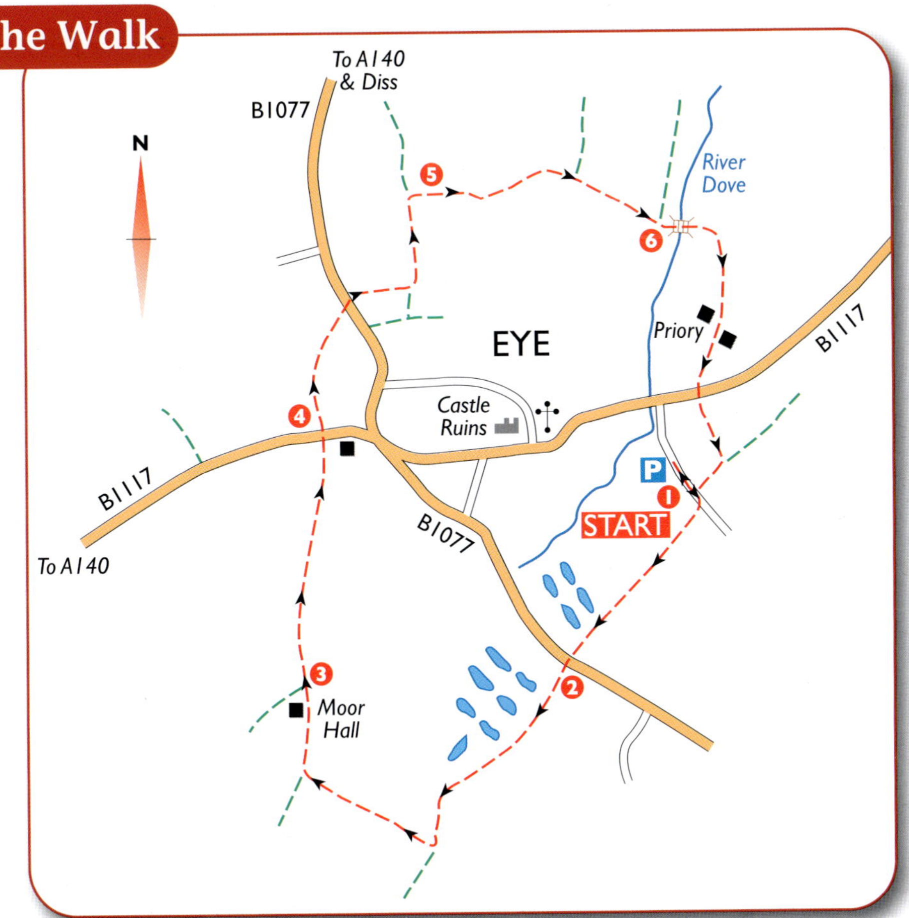

Kiddiwalks in Suffolk

Nature Reserve in Ludgate Causeway (GR 151737).
Map: OS Explorer 230 Diss & Harleston.
Refreshments There are a number of places in the village, including the Queens Head pub and the Lyndsay House restaurant. If you prefer to take a picnic, you will find tables in the nature reserve very close to the start of the walk.

1 Turn right out of the car park and walk along a leafy lane. When you reach the houses, take the footpath on the right after house number 3 and go over a little stile by the metal gate. Follow the grass path, which is part of the Mid-Suffolk Footpath, by grazing fields and two large ponds. Continue on until you reach the unusual carved tree trunk by the road.

2 Cross the road and take the footpath opposite along Park Lane. Go around the metal barrier and along the private road, which is a public right of way. Pass more ponds and when you reach the footpath junction, turn right over the stile. Pass a fallen tree and cross the concrete bridge. Continue through the grass fields until you come to a wooden bridge. Turn right, heading towards the church. Keep to the left side of the field and go over the stile by the old wooden barn building, part of Moor Hall.

◆ Fun Things to See and Do ◆

This is an ideal walk for learning to **identify the native English trees**. The children could collect leaves from the many different trees that you pass whilst walking and when they get home they can make them into a collage and label each one. Oak, elm, ash, horse-chestnut, beech, sycamore and hawthorn are just some of the trees found growing along the way. In winter time, the trees can be identified by their shape and bark, as well as by the fruit (such as acorns) which are left scattered on the ground.

If you take a detour into the town at point 4, the children can enjoy climbing up to the **ruined castle**.

3 Proceed along the farm track, which bends right. Soon after the bend look out for a footpath post tucked away in the hedge on the left. This soon takes you into a wood, which provides another chance to collect leaves. Stay right after the concrete bridge, pass a pond then cross over a little railway sleeper bridge. At the next junction of paths, go right over another concrete bridge and into a grass meadow, called Town Moor. Go alongside the football pitch and through the gap by the children's playground to the road where the crinkle crankle wall can be seen.

4 To visit the centre of Eye and the castle at this stage, go right; but to continue the walk, take the footpath directly opposite on the other side of the road. Pass a house and proceed along a grass path, which soon converts to a dirt track and bends right to the next road. Turn left and then immediately right on the other side of the road along a concrete path. Follow the line of the stream, going through a metal swing gate to the cycle track. Go left up the track and at the next junction with the road turn right.

5 Proceed through the residential area, passing Maple

The wooden sculpture passed on the route

Way, to the end of the road. At the 'Ash Road' sign go left to the garages. Just the other side of the row of garages you will see a stile. Go over this and walk straight across the open field (there may be no defined path here), heading to the left of the telegraph post on the other side. Where the hedgerow ends on the other side, bear right along the field edge, keeping the hedge and ditch to the left. Ahead is a red-brick building, part of the old priory. Go gently downhill to the corner of the field and go over the stile by the metal gate.

6 Follow the concrete path over the bridge, which crosses the River Dove. It bends gradually right past the priory and an information board which tells you all about it. When you reach the road, the footpath entrance is just to the left of the large metal gates and you follow the grand drive as far as the bend, where you go right over a stile. Cross the field and go over another stile. This soon takes you to the lane by Oak House. Turn right, back along the lane, and the car park is further down the road on the left.

◆ Background Notes ◆

The name 'Eye' comes from an Old English word meaning 'island', which suggests that the town was once entirely surrounded by water from the River Dove and its tributaries. A **castle was built at Eye** after the Norman Conquest by the Malet family who also founded the priory. It was twice sacked during the medieval period and for 400 years it was used as a prison, until the early 17th century when it fell into disrepair and much of its stone was taken away by the locals for building material. A windmill stood on the top of the mound until 1844 when the owner constructed a false keep, the remains of which survive today. The children can climb to the top where there is an excellent view of Eye and, in particular, the magnificent 14th-century church of St Peter and St Paul nearby. Other notable features of the town include a section of a **crinkle crankle wall**, which you pass on the way (see also Walk 15 at Easton), the **almshouses** (almost opposite the wall) and the **town hall**, both built in Victorian times, and the 15th-century guildhall near the church.

The **wood carving** en route (at the end of point 1) is a 10 ft head carving in oak by Ray Brooks of Treesculpture, a company based in a sawmill near Coney Weston in Suffolk.

The **Pennings Nature Reserve** at the start of the route contains meadows with a variety of wild flowers and bird life and is well worth exploring.

Stonham Aspal

Mythical Creatures and Ten Bells

Here is a walk around the quaint village of Stonham Aspal. You can choose the longer route, which leads you through the quiet countryside to the south, or take a shortcut along the village street. There is also the option of walking to the Stonham Barns attraction, which has plenty to entertain the youngsters. In any case, whatever your choice, you will encounter some grand old farm halls along the way.

Kiddiwalks in Suffolk

10

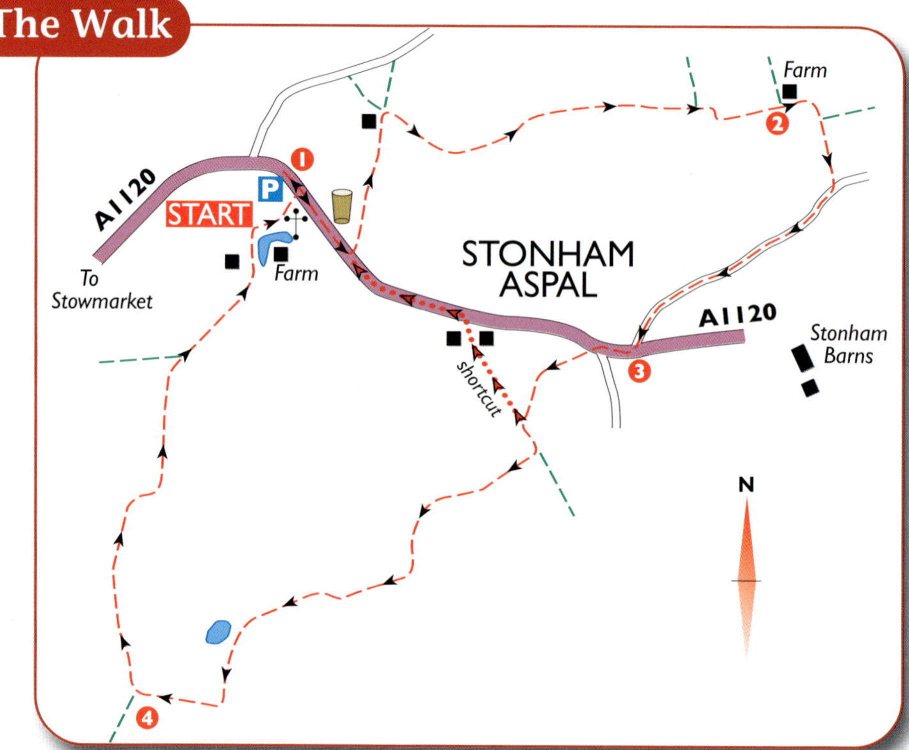

Getting there *Stonham Aspal lies on the A1120, east of Stowmarket.*

Length of walk 2¼ or 3½ miles.
Time 1 or 1¾ hours.
Terrain Very flat and easy walking with wide footpaths for much of the distance. There are no stiles. The shorter route is ideal for pushchairs.
Start/Parking In the village hall free car park next to the church at the west end of the village (GR 133595).
Map: OS Explorer 211 Bury St Edmunds & Stowmarket.
Refreshments The Ten Bells opposite the church, near the start of the walk, is a very children-friendly pub with a pleasant garden. At Stonham Barns there are the Barn Tea Rooms.

The Walk

1 Walk along the main road into the village, passing the primary school and the church. About 50 yards after the Ten Bells pub, take the footpath on the left. At the house keep right; the public footpath goes into a large field with a hedge and ditch to the left. Go gently down and through a gap at the bottom, turning right on the other side. This path continues for some distance to the end of the field. Go through the gap on the right and bear left so that the ditch is now on your left. The path is a good wide grass path. Proceed straight on to Goldings Farm, which you can see ahead of you.

2 When you reach the farm garden, cross the wooden bridge on the right, over the brook, and go left on the other side of the bridge, past the cottage. At the end of the hedge, go through the wooden gate and out onto the drive. Turn right onto the drive, which takes you to a little lane. Here turn right along the lane,

◆ Fun Things to See and Do ◆

At the church, which is usually open, there are **carved animals and creatures** at both ends of the unusual wooden pews inside. See if you can identify them all, but it's not easy to do because some of the carvings are not of real animals at all, but mythical creatures with wings. The church also has an old 8-ft **iron chest** that is so heavy that pulleys are needed to lift it.

Stonham Barns is situated a mile further east down the main road from the church (or reached from the walk – see point 3). Here there are all sorts of things to do for all the family. Admission to the main complex is free and so is parking. There is a bird of prey centre and owl sanctuary with over 70 birds (telephone: 01449 711425). There is also a children's playground, crazy putting and pitch and putt for the older children, a children's animal petting farm and a fish and reptile shop. And for mum and dad, there are lots of craft shops, an antique centre and a garden centre.

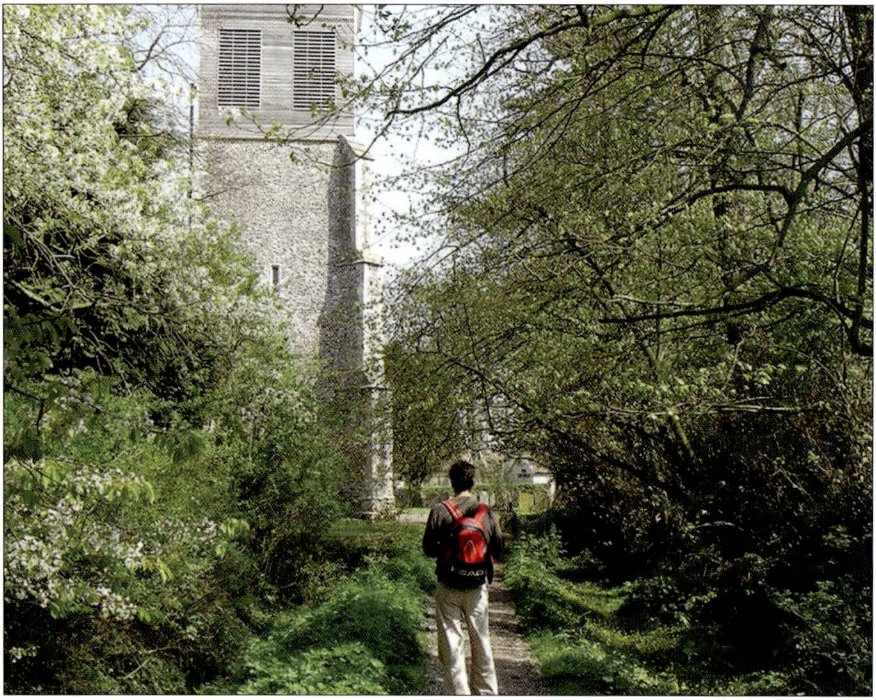

passing houses and the pink-coloured Longlands Hall and continuing to the main road. (*If you wish to walk to Stonham Barns, turn left here along the grass verge and the barns are about five minutes' walk, on the right-hand side.*)

3 Turn right and shortly after the road junction, turn left along a footpath leading to the recreation ground. Follow alongside the football pitch as far as the corner.

For the shortcut, just before you reach the corner of the pitch, go through the gap in the hedge on the right, taking you along a clear path across the field, then between the houses and down an alley to the main road. Here turn left and walk along the pavement through the village. You will have to cross the road where the walkway runs out and use the pavement on the other side. This will take you directly to the church and the village hall.

For the main route, go left along

by the next pitch and when you reach the farm track at the footpath crossroads, turn right. The path bends left then right. At the junction go left (the right option is a private track and not a public footpath) and the path winds along and takes a sharp right, leading to a path T-junction where there is a thicket and an old tree stump.

4 Turn right along a path, which is a little narrow. It bends 90° to the right and soon after you go left across the ditch on an unmarked path heading uphill. Proceed to the top and at the footpath T-junction, go right. Bear left at the footpath marker post along the farm track but before you reach the hay-barn go right, across the meadow and through the open metal gates. Go alongside the barbed wire fence towards the church. Pass through another metal gate by the brook and you will see, to your right, the wonderful old moated farmhouse of Broughton Hall. At the footpath sign turn right and go along a track with a ditch either side, leading to the church. Go through the churchyard to the road, where you turn left to return to the village hall.

◆ Background Notes ◆

The pub gets its name from the ten bells that ring from the wooden bell tower in the **church of St Mary and St Lambert** opposite. It is unusual for a church to have as many as ten bells. But in 1742 Squire Ecclestone of Crowfield, who was a keen bell-ringer himself, decided to have the then five bells increased to ten. He lopped off the top of the flint tower and replaced it with a wooden bell tower in order to house the bells. The poppy-headed bench ends have magnificent carvings. Two in the chancel have splendid arm-rest figures of an angel, an eagle, a winged lion and a winged bull; sixteen in the nave (some carved by villagers still living) have a griffin, an eagle, lions, praying figures, and a wolf guarding the head of St Edmund.

The **Mid Suffolk Showground** is situated at Stonham Barns and holds various special events throughout the year. Telephone: 01449 711755.

11

Bramford

Compass Fun

Just to the west of Ipswich lie two little communities that have managed to retain their village atmosphere. Bramford and Sproughton are connected by road, rail and river. This walk starts by the railway in Bramford and follows the River Gipping to Sproughton before returning through some lovely countryside to the west. Use this route to encourage children to learn how to take compass readings as they journey around.

Getting there *Leave the A14 at the Sproughton junction. At the village centre go right along the B1113 and turn right into Bramford village then right again, onto the B1067 towards Ipswich. The parking area is on the right just before the railway line.*

Length of walk 3½ miles.
Time 1¾ hours.
Terrain No stiles to negotiate. There is one short stretch of busy road at point 2 of the walk and a little road walking mostly along quiet lanes.
Start/Parking In the free car park next to the railway line in Bramford (GR 128465).
Map: OS Explorer 197 Ipswich, Felixstowe & Harwich.

Refreshments There are two pubs en route: the Wild Man in Sproughton and, near the end of the walk, the excellent Bramford Cock, which is ideal for children as it has a garden playground. There is also a picnic area at the start of the walk by the car park.
NB: For (C) see **Fun Things to See and Do**.

1 From the rear of the car park, go through the wooden gate onto the little path leading away from the railway line towards the church. Turn left just before the river and follow the path along by the river bank. Old Bramford village can be seen on the other side of the river to your right. Go over a concrete bridge, then over two more bridges before the path

◆ Fun Things to See and Do ◆

Where you see the (C) sign in the walk directions, the children could take a **compass reading**. There will be different readings throughout the journey. The younger ones can learn the four compass directions, North, South, East and West, and they can point in the direction of each.

Ducks and swans can often be seen on the river so if you take some bread and tasty morsels with you, the children can feed them.

The Walk

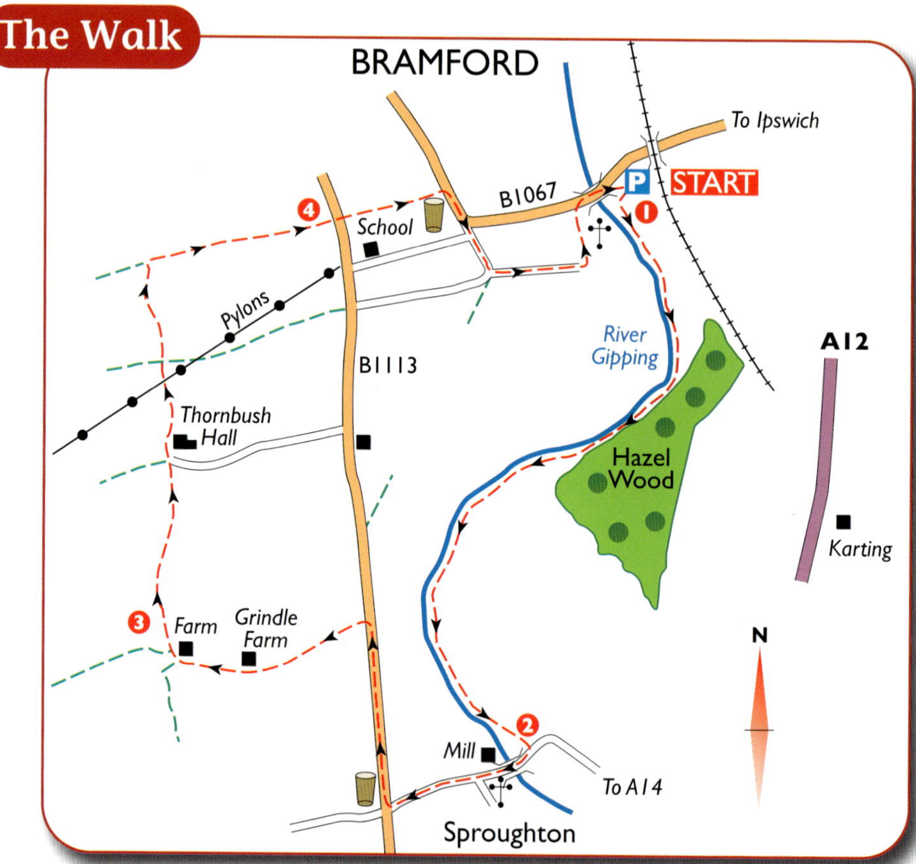

swings to the right along a raised stretch of the path, between the river and Hazel Wood. (C) Continue to follow this river path all the way to Sproughton Lock. Here you cross over a bridge and go up the steps to the road.

2 Turn right past the church on the left and the old Sproughton Mill building to your right.

Proceed up to the junction at the Wild Man pub. Go right and travel along the footway, which runs parallel to the main road. (C) After about ¼ mile, you will need to cross the busy road, taking the track on the left, which leads to Grindle Farm. Go up the track with its pretty brook that runs alongside (C) until you reach the house at the top.

3 Go right and bear right again along a wide dirt track towards Thornbush Hall, which you can see ahead on the hill. When you reach the buildings at Thornbush Hall go straight on at the footpath junction, and as you pass the hay barn, go right and left by the farm buildings, and then gently uphill along a tractor path by the side of the field. Then out onto open farmland with beautiful views of the Suffolk countryside all around. (C) Take a compass reading as you pass under the pylons. At the T-junction by the footpath post, turn right and proceed downhill towards the church in the distance. You arrive at the main road.

4 Go straight across, down a tarmac path along by the school. (C) At the next road turn right, passing the Bramford Cock pub, and at the road junction, go straight on along Fitzgerald Road and then left down Vicarage Lane. Go past the old vicarage and at the churchyard turn left through a swing gate along a path by the church. Turn right along by the red-brick wall of the church grounds and left out of the church gate to the main road. Turn right and, straight after the bridge, right again down the steps and left along the little path that takes you back to the car park.

◆ Background Notes ◆

The **River Gipping** runs through Bramford and Sproughton and between 1793 and 1830 it used to take barges carrying all sorts of goods between Ipswich and Stowmarket. The **old mill at Sproughton**, built in the 1800s, would have used the river to carry its grain and flour but today the mill and the lock lie disused. The railways were the reason for the decline of the barges on the river.

Along the 17-mile-long **Gipping Valley River Path**, where you start the walk, there are information boards that point out the black poplar, which grows by the river, Britain's rarest native timber tree. They also have information about the bush crickets that can be found by the river in summer and the otters that have been spotted close by.

Stutton

Water, Water, Everywhere

There is something restful and pleasing about walking alongside open water and children never fail to enjoy it. This circuit starts from the tranquil Alton Water reservoir and follows the path along by this large lake for a while. It then swings through farmland to the village of Stutton and along a country lane with distant views of the River Stour, before passing the majestic Royal Hospital School and back to the Alton Water Country Park.

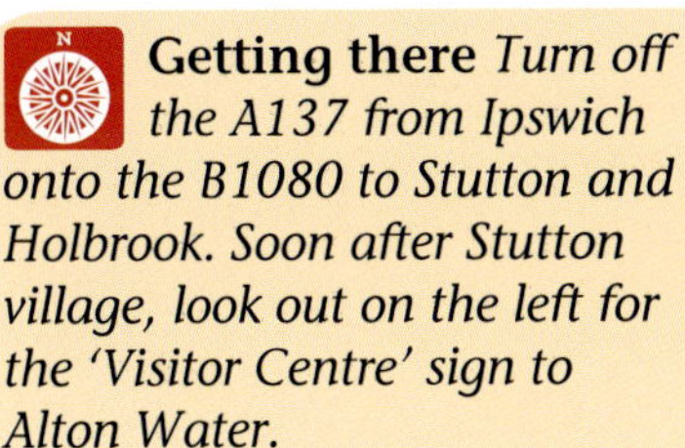

Getting there *Turn off the A137 from Ipswich onto the B1080 to Stutton and Holbrook. Soon after Stutton village, look out on the left for the 'Visitor Centre' sign to Alton Water.*

Length of walk 3¾ miles.
Time 2 hours.
Terrain There are a couple of stiles to negotiate, as well as a little road walking along quiet lanes, plus a short stretch along a main road on the last stretch of the circuit where there is a good pavement.

Start/Parking: The country park pay and display car park (all-day tickets available) next to the visitor centre (GR 157353).

Map OS Explorer 197 Ipswich, Felixstowe & Harwich.

Refreshments The café at the

The Walk

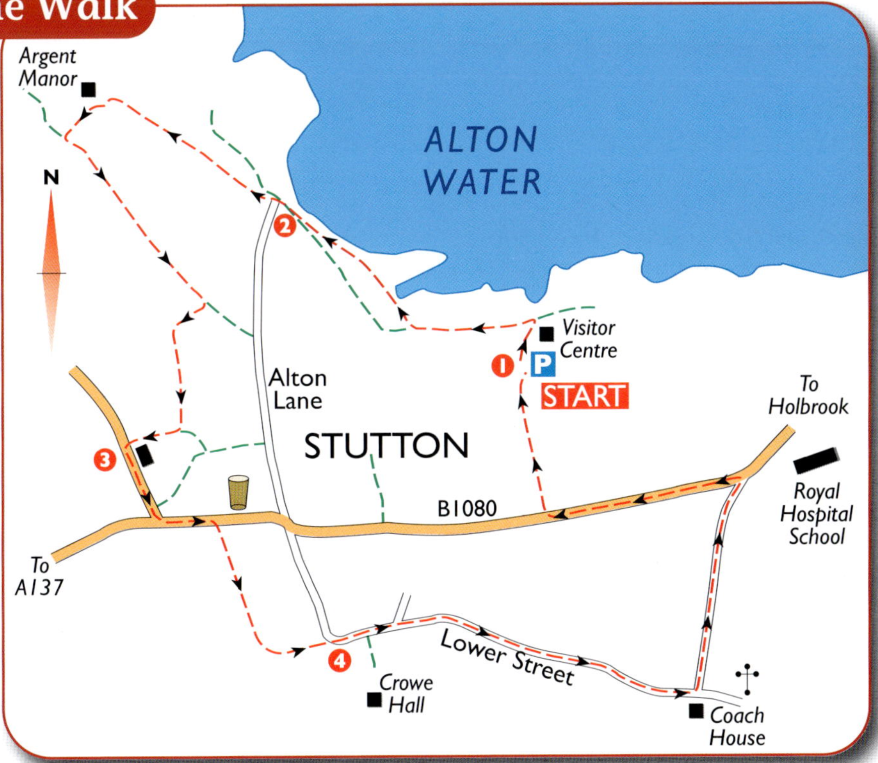

visitor centre offers light snacks. The 16th-century Kings Head pub en route in Stutton, which provides a full menu and has a seating area outside, welcomes children.

1 Go over the zebra crossing next to the visitor centre and follow the dirt track, which runs alongside Alton Water. Bear right to follow the grass path that runs closer to the reservoir. Just before it rejoins the dirt track, turn right towards the reservoir and then left when you reach the water. Continue left along the path next to the reservoir. Enjoy the views across the water. When you reach the red lifebuoy, turn left up to the wooden shelter (which provides information about the wildlife around the lake).

2 Go through the gap in the fence leading to the lane that runs away from the reservoir, but turn immediately right by the metal gate, onto the footpath running through the young saplings. Continue on between the horse fields to Argent Manor. Here you turn left over a stile and soon after go over a second stile by the horse field. At the corner, turn left, still following the fence, and at the next corner, go straight on, across the open field. There is no defined path across this field but keep in a straight line to the hedge. Turn right on the other side of the hedge and follow the path to the footpath junction shortly after where the corner of three fields meet. Go left, along by the oak trees and further down a hedge. When you reach the footpath signpost at the end of the field, turn right and this will take you to the road.

◆ Fun Things to See and Do ◆

Alton Water is an excellent place for **spotting water birds** – take some binoculars along with you if possible. You can view them from the lakeside or from undercover in one of the many bird hides. Take along a fishing net and a jam jar too so that the children can try **dipping into the reservoir** to see what can be found living in the water.

3 Turn left along the road and at the T-junction turn left again along the B1080 for a short distance. Almost opposite the Kings Head pub, turn right along a narrow path between the houses. The path diverts through the hedge and at the end of the field you turn left. The path becomes wider and then joins the lane called Lower Street.

4 Go straight on towards the church, passing the entrance to Crowe Hall. At the junction by the Coach House go left (*to visit the parish church go straight on before returning here*) and proceed to the end of the little lane, back to the main road where there is a good view of the Royal Hospital School. Turn left back along the main road, using the walkway on the other side, and turn right back to the Alton Water Visitor Centre where you started.

◆ Background Notes ◆

Alton Water, the largest area of inland water in Suffolk, was opened in 1987 by the Princess Royal. Alton Hall now lies beneath the reservoir and Alton Mill was dismantled and rebuilt at the Museum of East Anglian Life in Stowmarket. Many sporting activities are possible in the country park, including sailing, windsurfing and fishing, and there are also dragon boats. Much wildlife can be found on and around the lake, and bird hides are situated all around the reservoir. And, of course, many people come to Alton Water to walk and picnic. As well as the café, the visitor centre provides cycle hire and toilets.

The **Royal Hospital School** is located between Stutton and Holbrook towards the end of the route. Its tower, which can be seen from miles around, acts as a landmark during the walk. The school was founded in 1714 as part of the Greenwich Hospital and is the oldest Military School in the country. Due to expansion the site was moved to its present location in 1933. It is still very much associated with its maritime heritage; pupils, who board there, are issued with a naval uniform and their education includes navigation and sailing training.

Chelmondiston

From Little Acorns ...

Admiring the River Orwell

This walk has the option of a short walk or a longer one but both enjoy the picturesque backdrop of the River Orwell. Pin Mill is a very small riverside hamlet consisting of a few houses, a pub and the boatyards at the end of the lane, half a mile from the village of Chelmondiston and about seven miles downstream from Ipswich. It is an area of outstanding natural beauty, surrounded by National Trust woodlands and the river, which is about half a mile wide at Pin Mill. At low tide it's possible to walk out along the hard to the centre of the river to look upstream to the Orwell Bridge, just south of Ipswich.

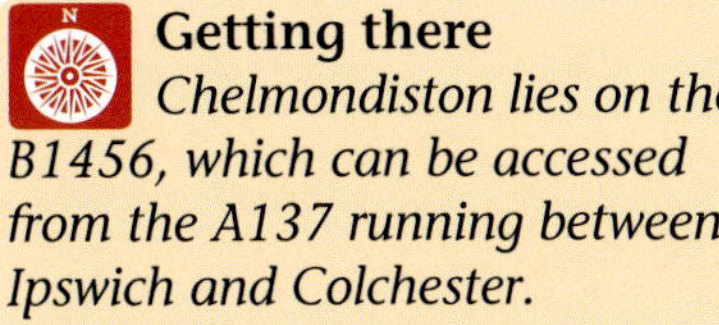

Getting there
Chelmondiston lies on the B1456, which can be accessed from the A137 running between Ipswich and Colchester.
Turn off the B1456 into Pin Mill Road.

Length of walk 1½ or 3¼ miles.
Time ¾ hour or 1¾ hours.
Terrain There are a couple of stiles to negotiate, as well as a little road walking at the start of the walk.
Start/Parking In the pay and display car park near the end of Pin Mill Road (GR 206378). If this is full there is the option of parking at the free car park up on the main road next to the post office, which will add ¼ mile to your walk.
Map OS Explorer 197 Ipswich, Felixstowe & Harwich.
Refreshments Pin Mill is a good place to take a picnic as there are two picnic sites near the start/finish of the walk. Alternatively, there is the popular Butt and Oyster where you can sit outside overlooking the river. It is said that yachtsmen can be served with pints of ale through the windows of the pub at high tide.

1 Turn left out of the car park and walk down the road towards the River Orwell. Go to the Butt

◆ Fun Things to See and Do ◆

Measuring the old oak towards the end of point 2. If you join hands around the tree with your arms spread horizontally, it is possible to measure the circumference of this huge oak. When you get home, measure everyone's arm-span and total them up to find an approximate distance for the circumference of the tree. It is said that if you measure the tree in centimetres and divide by 2.5, this gives you the age of the tree in years.

If there are any **acorns** lying on the ground, why not take one home and plant it in a pot? Keep the pot watered and you may find an oak tree growing in time.

13

The Walk

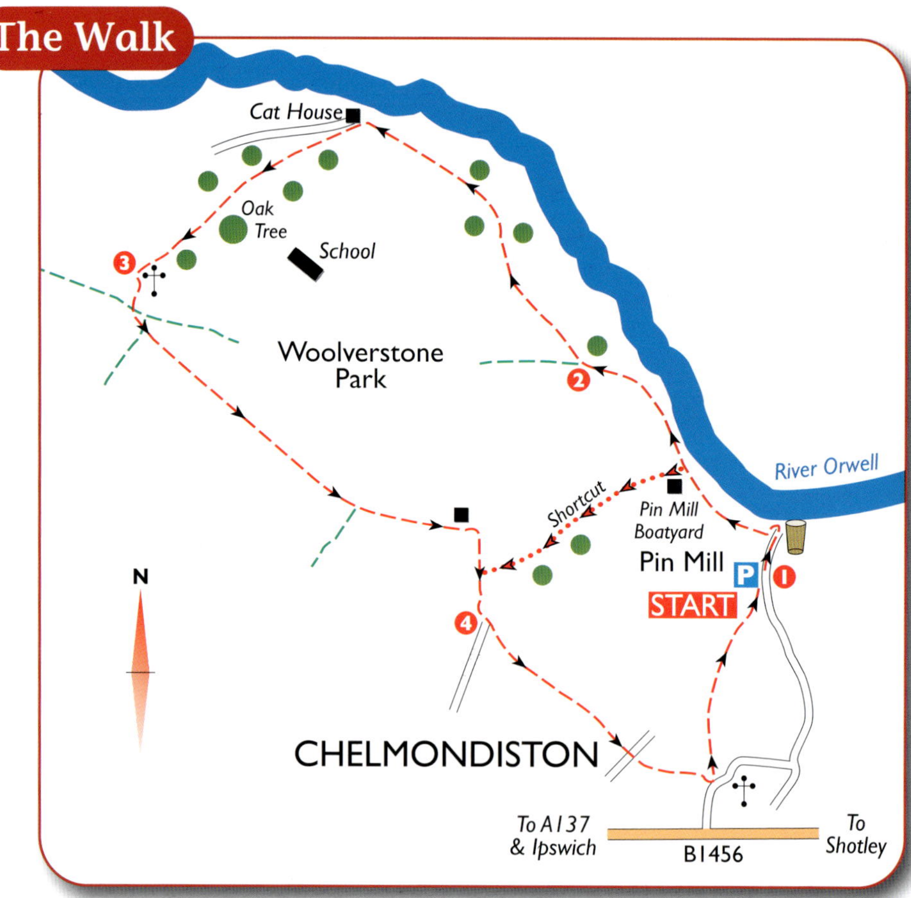

and Oyster pub at the end and turn left. Soon after, bear left up a bridleway by Pin Mill Sailing Club, then turn right at the garages, also a bridleway. Continue to the next junction*.

For the short walk, leave the main route here by turning left up by the boatyard onto a stony path. Continue uphill on a wide track, alongside a wooded area where the path loses its stones. At the junction you turn left, rejoining the main route at point 4.

For the full walk, at * go straight on, taking you closer to the river. Go over a tiny bridge and proceed along by the meadow. At the large oak, where

the path forks, keep right across the field.

2 The path soon bends right towards the river, then along a winding path running parallel to the water. Continue on to the Royal Harwich Yacht Club. Follow the footpath arrows round to the pier, where you turn left onto a concrete track. Opposite Cat House watch out for the footpath arrow on the post of the corner of the marina car park, taking you left into the woods. The path winds this way and that, going gently uphill through the trees and the bracken. You will pass by a very old massive oak tree on

your way up to the church and the recreation ground.

3 Follow the path around the church to the entrance, where you are forced right. There are two consecutive stiles on the left. Take the second one, going across a field to a double stile. Cross School Road – this goes to Ipswich High School, which can be seen in the distance – and across a little field. Go over the next stile into a field with a good path alongside. A water tower can be seen to the left. Continue past two large oaks to a wide farm track by the cottage. Continue straight on along the track alongside a holly hedge. The track then bends right. At the bridleway go straight on down the track and back up again.

4 Watch out for the bridleway turning on the left, taking you into a meadow. In the distance is the river, and Orwell Park House can be seen beyond. Proceed on past a children's playground.

Continue across the road (Collimer Close) and at the next road head towards the church. Just before the T-junction, turn left down the bridleway towards Pin Mill. Go downhill towards the river. Go over a stile and down a pleasant grass path. Take the second stile on the left, which will take you back to the Pin Mill car park.

◆ Background Notes ◆

Pin Mill attracts many visitors throughout the year and it is especially popular with walkers, artists and lovers of wildlife, especially birdwatchers. But, traditionally, the most frequent visitors coming to Pin Mill are the sailors and the boat enthusiasts who take advantage of the natural harbour and the facilities along the Orwell. There is a boatyard and a sailing club. Boat-builders, boat houses, yachtsmen and visiting craft such as Thames barges make this stretch of the river a hive of activity for most of the year.

The **Orwell Bridge** has the biggest single span of concrete in England and carries traffic from Felixstowe docks to the rest of the country.

The **oak tree** is the most popular of our native species, and so it is considered as our national tree. It is deciduous, shedding its leaves in autumn, and the acorn is its fruit. It is very hardy and versatile, and its wood is used for building ships and houses (see Walk 8, Stoke by Nayland). Oaks grow to great heights and can live for hundreds of years.

Dendrochronology is the name given to the method of dating timber by studying the pattern of the tree's ring growth. The children can impress their friends with this word!

Felixstowe Ferry

Guarding the Shore

Having fun on the beach

Felixstowe is the largest container port in the United Kingdom. Some 2 miles to the north-east is the little fishing hamlet called Felixstowe Ferry. Here there are two Martello towers, a boatyard and a ferry across the river in the summer months. The ships that sail into and out of the port can often be seen from this part of the coast. Starting on the outskirts of Felixstowe, the walk takes a route around the golf course, at first following a shore-side path to the ferry and then a permissive path further inland on the way back. If you are able to take the ferry trip over to the Bawdsey Peninsula at the halfway point, you will have the opportunity to enjoy an ice cream on the beach.

14

Getting there *The A14 goes to Felixstowe. As you approach the town at the first roundabout, take the first exit following Candlet Road, the A154, and continue on the A1021 at the next roundabout. At the third roundabout take the last exit continuing on the A1021, then at the next roundabout take the first exit onto High Road East. Continue onto Cliff Road and the entrance to the car park is on the right.*

Length of walk 2¼ miles.
Time 1¼ hours.
Terrain Flat, easy walking along good paths. There is a combination of public rights of way and a permissive path. If you can negotiate the steps (see point 1), it would be possible to take a pushchair on this walk.
Start/Parking In the Clifflands pay and display car park (GR 323363).
Map OS Explorer 197 Ipswich, Felixstowe & Harwich.
Refreshments The Ferry Boat Inn and the Ferry Café. If you take the ferry across to Bawdsey Quay, there is a café by the beach.

1 Take the path from the car park past the information board, leading towards the beach. Descend the steps and turn left

◆ Fun Things to See and Do ◆

If you're here when it's running, **catch the ferry**, which shuttles across the River Deben to Bawdsey Quay, taking just minutes to reach its destination. On the other side is a safe little beach where the children can play and paddle if the weather is kind.

On the way round, as you walk along the promenade you will see some smaller boats and watercraft and you will also pass the boatyards. Take some binoculars and see if the youngsters can make out the **names on the side of the boats**. Older children could write them down and everyone could have fun deciding what name they would choose for a boat of their own. The favourite one I spotted was *Wotdat*.

The Walk

along the beach path. To the left is the golf course and further along, a Martello tower. The hard surface converts to a wide sand and stone path. Watch the activity out to sea – the boats and large ships heading to and from Felixstowe port, and the sailing craft. Continue past a second Martello tower, this one converted into a home. At the Ferry Yacht Club, bear left, taking the steps down to the road. For a ferry trip turn right; otherwise, cross

One of the Martello towers passed along the way

straight over the road along the footpath.

2 Proceed along a raised concrete path, which runs alongside the boatyard with its yachts and houseboats. There is an alternative lower grass path if you need shelter. At the junction at the end, go left along the permissive Tomline path through the golf course, probably named after George Tomline, the second largest landowner in Suffolk during the latter part of the 19th century. This is a raised grass path that meanders along by the golf course with more distant views of the Martello towers to the left and pleasant views of the countryside to the right. Next to the 3rd tee there is an old seat if you require a rest.

3 Cross the private track and continue to the end of the path, which passes through a thicket and out to the road through a wooden swing gate. Turn left along the road for a short distance then, at the footpath sign, turn right across the golf course. Head for the footpath post and then continue to the sea wall. Turn right and retrace your route along the seafront to the steps back up to the car park.

◆ Background Notes ◆

Coastal defence has been a high priority for hundreds of years in Felixstowe. Further down the coast, guarding the main port is Languard Fort and there are many Second World War fortifications and pillboxes. But along this route are two **Martello towers**, built to help repel an invasion from Napoleon Bonaparte in the early 19th century. In 1805 Bonaparte controlled much of Europe, so in preparation for the defence of the realm, it was decided to construct a chain of towers along the east and south coast of England, the area most vulnerable to attack. These were called Martello towers, named after an attack on the town of Mortella in Italy when the Royal Navy was repulsed by a similar structure. In total 105 were built and 47 of them survive today. The two towers along this stretch of coast were constructed between 1800 and 1815 and contain 8 ft thick walls. These structures usually contained two floors and from the top they have extensive views across the sea. Cannon were mounted on the top. Today, one tower stands redundant and the other one has been converted into a family home.

There has been a **ferry across to the Bawdsey Peninsula** for over a hundred years, taking foot passengers over the River Deben and providing continuity for the Suffolk Coast and Heaths Path. The owner of Bawdsey Manor, Sir William Quilter, operated a steam-drawn chain ferry in 1894. It was temporarily closed during the Second World War but was re-introduced by the RAF when the war was over. Today the ferry operates at weekends from Easter to the end of April and daily from May to October. There is a small charge. Telephone: 01394 282173; mobile 07709 411511.

Bawdsey Manor was a top secret Radar research centre during the Second World War.

Easton

A Crinkle Crankle Experience

Easton is situated in the gentle valley of the River Deben. It is a very pretty village and the unusual crinkle crankle wall that can be seen on the walk is just one of its distinctive features. The river is crossed at the start of the circuit and then the path goes out into the beautiful countryside that surrounds the village. Easton Farm Park, passed at point 2 of the walk, is one of the best children's attractions in Suffolk.

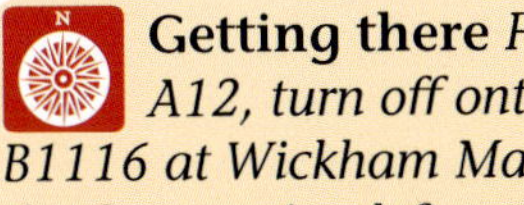

Getting there *From the A12, turn off onto the B1116 at Wickham Market, then the first turning left onto Easton Road. At the next junction, turn right into Wickham Market Road, which will take you into the centre of the village.*

Length of walk 3¼ miles.
Time 1¾ hours.
Terrain A straightforward walk with no stiles and good wide footpaths, with a short section on a straight road.
Start/Parking In the free car park almost opposite the White Horse pub in the centre of the village (GR 284586).
Map OS Explorer 212 Woodbridge & Saxmundham.
Refreshments The White Horse Inn at the start of the walk has a very pleasant garden at the back with chickens. There is a tearoom at Easton Farm Park.

◆ Fun Things to See and Do ◆

On the way round the children can count the number of 'waves' in the **crinkle crankle wall**. There are two opportunities to see the wall, at the very start of the walk soon after you emerge from the car park and again when you come to the road in point 3 of the walk. It might be interesting to count the number of brick courses at each of these locations to see if the wall is the same height.

Easton Farm Park is a well-established tourist attraction, specifically organised with children of all ages in mind. There are pony & cart rides and train rides. You can feed and stroke the animals. There is an indoor soft play area, face-painting and an adventure playground. Details of opening times and admission charges are on the website www.eastonfarmpark.co.uk or you could telephone 01728 746475.

A few miles to the north is the appealing town of **Framlingham**, with its ancient castle; this is open to visitors and regular special events are held in the grounds.

15

The Walk

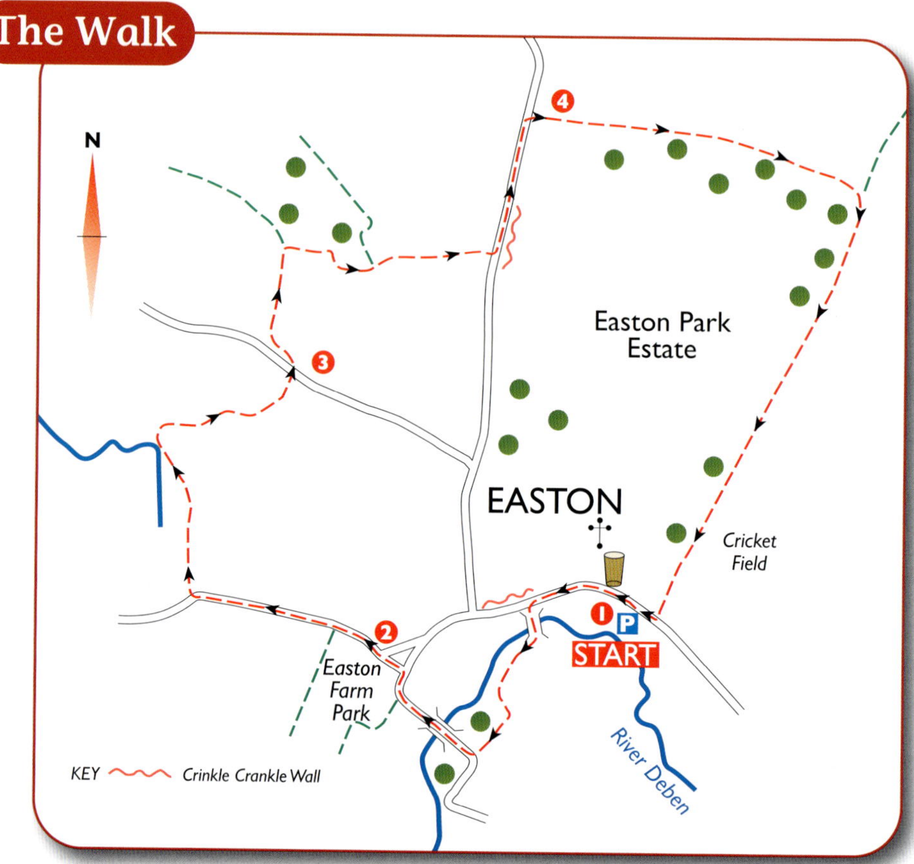

1 From the car park, turn left past the quaint White Horse Inn. The road bends left. Just after the Easton Harriers Hunt Kennels, take the footpath on the left. Go over the bridge, where you are forced right, then over two more bridges as you continue through the trees. When you cross the next bridge you walk out onto a farm track, which leads to the lane. Turn right over the road bridge and at the next road junction turn left towards Hoo and Monewden.

2 Continue down the lane past the entrance to Easton Farm Park. At the second hedgerow on the right at the bottom of the dip, take the footpath on the right along a wide grass field-edge

path. When you reach the ditch at the end of the field, do not cross it but turn right, staying in the same field and going gently uphill. At the brow of the slope the path bends 90° left, soon taking you to the road.

3 Take the footpath opposite, going up the bank and left along the field edge. On the other side of the next hedgerow, turn right along another wide grass path. At the footpath junction by the wood, turn right. The path follows around the edge of the wood and continues to the road. Opposite is a section of crinkle crankle wall. Turn left along the road, keeping on the verge where you can. Pass Stable Cottage and when you see the red postbox by the side of the road, turn right along the footpath, which is tucked away and running between the fences.

4 Go around the old oak and over the footbridge and continue along by the wood. When you eventually reach the footpath signs at the junction, go right. The wood is still to the right and a crop field to the left. Continue down this long straight path for some distance. You will pass the cricket field and bowling green and then go down a track leading to the road in the village. Turn right and you will see the car park ahead of you on the left side of the road.

15

◆ Background Notes ◆

The village of Easton has a grand church, a good pub and is well known for the famous park on its doorstep. The **crinkle crankle, or serpentine, wall**, which can be seen in the village and along parts of the walk, used to be the perimeter wall to the large estate and was built in 1830. Although the house on the estate, Easton Hall, was later pulled down, large sections of the wall survive. It is distinctive because it is built with the characteristic bendy, snake-like curves, which make it strong and obviate the need for buttresses.

The **Victorian buildings of Easton Farm Park** are what remain of the model farm for the Easton Estate, which was owned by the Duke and Duchess of Hamilton in the 19th century. When it became redundant as a working farm in 1970, it wasn't long before the site was converted to a farm park for families to enjoy.

Enjoying a ride at Easton Farm Park

Flixton

Woodland and flying machines

Some of the exhibits on display at the aviation museum

Flixton, close to the Norfolk border, is a very small community that is spread out and contains nothing much more than a church, a pub and a scattering of farms and cottages. This walk will be appreciated particularly by older children. It is a longer route and can include a visit to the excellent aviation museum, which the dads will enjoy too! The circuit starts from the museum and leads you south through woodland and over farmland before returning past the church and the Buck Inn.

16

Getting there *Flixton lies about 3 miles south-west of Bungay on the B1062 (off the A143), which runs between Bungay and Homersfield.*

Length of walk 3½ miles.
Time 1¾ hours.

Terrain There are no steep hills or stiles but there is a section of road walking that might not be suitable for tiny tots.

Start/Parking The free car park in front of the gates to the Norfolk and Suffolk Aviation Museum next to the pub (GR 312874).

The Walk

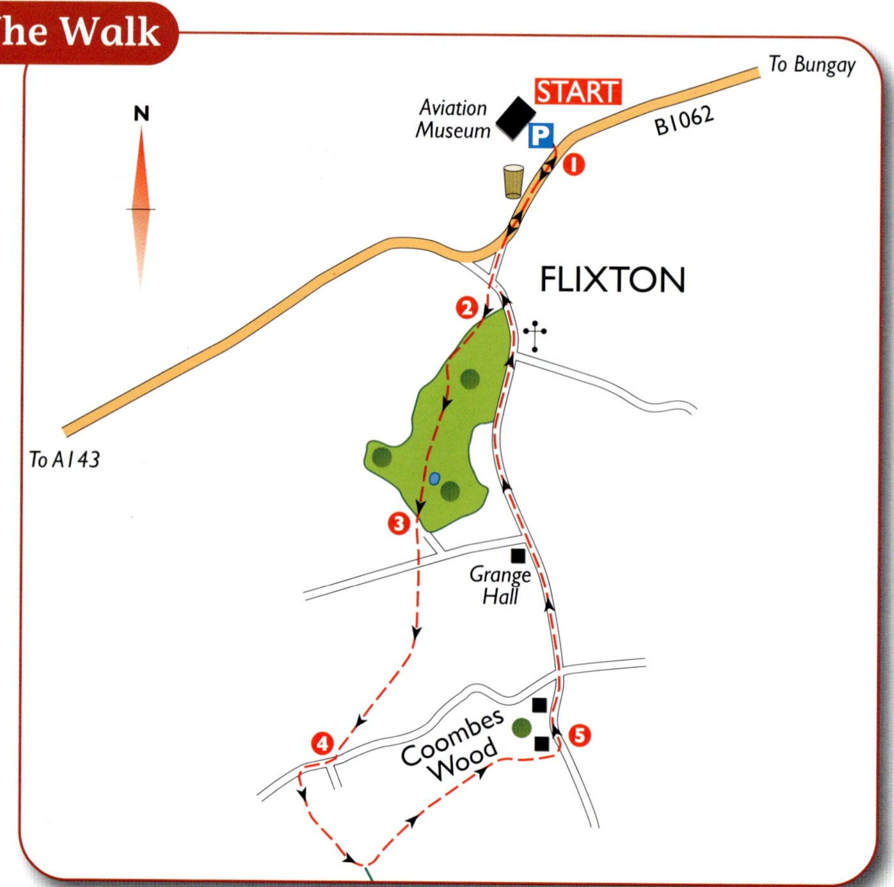

Map OS Explorer 231 Southwold & Bungay.

Refreshments The Buck Inn is next to the Aviation Museum where you park and there is a café inside the museum.

1 From the Aviation Museum, turn right along the road, which has a good pavement. At the road junction turn left towards South Elmham villages. Just before St Mary's Close, take the narrow footpath on the right. The path soon emerges into the countryside with a wood alongside to the left. Towards the end of the wood the path goes up a bank and across a grassy meadow. Keep to the left of the gymkhana area. Follow the yellow footpath signs into the wood.

2 The path winds around the trees. Go straight ahead at the next footpath post, along a straight double track. You have to keep your wits about you here because the path suddenly leaves the track and veers left through the woods – it is unmarked where it leaves the track and very difficult to spot. There is soon a large pond to be seen to the left. This takes you to a footpath post by the metal fence on the edge of the wood. Cross the wooden bridge and go through a metal gate into a grass meadow.

◆ Fun Things to See and Do ◆

The **woodland area** offers lots of opportunities for collecting leaves, for example, which can be pressed into a nature book at home and labelled (see Walk 9 at Eye). In the autumn there are acorns, conkers, sweet chestnuts and cones. See if the children can spot the fungi and mushrooms that grow in the ground and on the trees. These have wonderful names, like stinkhorn, witches' butter and ink cap, but they should never be picked as they may be poisonous.

Visit the Norfolk and Suffolk Aviation Museum. It is free to enter and there are many old aircraft exhibits both outside and under cover. For details, visit the website www.aviationmuseum.net or telephone 01986 896644.

3 Go left and head towards the corrugated barns. Just to the left of a brick ruin, go through another metal gate. Cross the farm track and take the footpath across the field. The path deviates slightly to the right and a long straight path cuts all the way across this very large field to the next metal gate. Bear left and about halfway along the hedge of the field you will be able to cross the brook and go out to the lane via an unusual metal gate.

4 Turn right along the lane and take the footpath you see signed on the left. It is a wide dirt track, which bends left. At the next footpath post go left, following a grass path that runs alongside a ditch. Continue straight on for some distance. At the end the path bends around the woods and some cottages to the road.

5 Turn left and at the next road junction go straight on. Proceed all the way down the road past Grange Hall to the next junction by the entrance to the church, which is on your right. Continue past the houses on a pavement returning you to the village sign, where you retrace your route at the beginning of the walk, turning right along the B1062 to return to the pub and the museum.

◆ Background Notes ◆

During the Second World War, East Anglia was an important strategic location for Royal Air Force bases, because it was so close to the German occupied European coast. Flixton was one such air base and today the remains of the runway can still be seen. The **aviation museum** was opened to the public in 1975 and is maintained and run mostly by volunteers. There are over sixty historic aircraft, including a Spitfire, a Sea Harrier, an English Electric Lightning and the reconstruction of an old First World War German Fokker. It also exhibits various themed collections, such as those of the Royal Observer Corps, RAF Bomber Command and the Air Sea Rescue and Coastal Command. Inside the large hangars can be seen old fire engines, many model planes and wartime pictures and mementos.

Halesworth

Under and Over

A pastoral scene at Halesworth

This varied route goes from the old market town of Halesworth to the village of Holton on its outskirts. The first half of the walk follows the banks of the pretty River Blyth as it meanders its way down towards the sea at Southwold. Because there are lots of irrigation channels and tributaries, many bridges have had to be constructed in order to access the footpath. You will get good views of Holton Windmill as you walk, and on your return to Halesworth the splendid little museum in the railway station is well worth a visit.

17

Getting there *Halesworth lies on the A144 between Bungay and the A12. From the A144 which runs through the town centre, turn off onto the B1124 towards Holton and then take the first turning left which is Station Road, a cul-de-sac leading to the station itself.*

Length of walk 3½ miles.
Time 1¾ hours.
Terrain No stiles and good grass paths for most of the journey but they are not very even in places so perhaps not a good route for pushchairs.

Start/Parking Free car parking outside Halesworth railway station near the town centre (GR 388778).

Map OS Explorer 231 Southwold & Bungay.

Refreshments There are several restaurants, cafés and pubs in the town, a few minutes away from the starting point.

1 Walk back down Station Road to the main road at the bottom and turn left at the T-junction.

◆ Fun Things to See and Do ◆

The children can **count the number of bridges** that they cross during their journey (there are lots on the first half of the walk). They could also keep a tally of the **number of gates** they pass through as well.

The **windmill** that can be seen along the way is open on the spring and August bank holidays. However, at any time of year you can take a small detour (see map, point 5) or go back to Holton later to view the exterior. Visitors can climb up the hill in the grounds of Mill House and look at this post mill at close quarters (for details of post mills, see Walk 18).

At the finishing point there is the free **museum** to visit and brass rubbings to be done (see 'Background Notes').

Oh, and there are always those **swing tyres** near the end of the route to play on!

The Walk

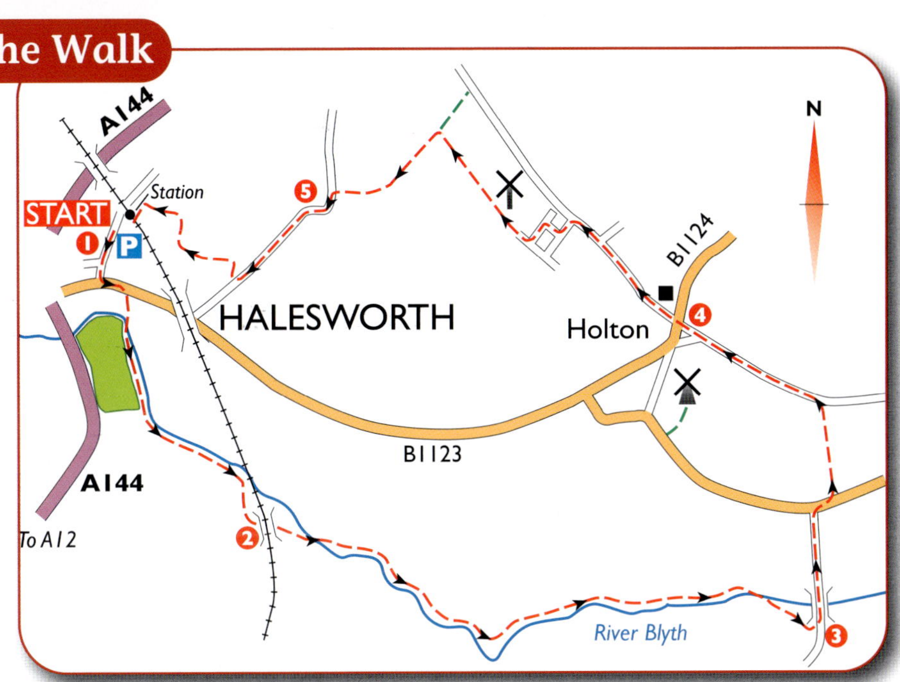

Just past the garage, turn right where you will see a footpath sign to 'Town Park'. Follow the high green metal fence, taking you across a bridge into the park. Go straight on past the skateboard play area and at the little path junction at the end turn left. At the river turn right. Follow this path along by the river. Go straight on at the next junction, through a wooden kissing gate and, soon after, go left through the next kissing gate, on a path that takes you through a tunnel under the railway line.

2 Go over a wooden bridge and through another wooden kissing gate. Bear left around the edge of the field by the barbed wire fence. After you pass under a little arch you are guided left over the stream. The route now follows along the other side of the river. Pass over a wooden bridge. At the next bridge with a wooden gate at the end go left across a meadow. You then go over another bridge into the next field where there is a good view of Holton Windmill in the distance to the left. Continue to follow the path by the river. Pass through another metal-gated bridge then a metal gate and then another bridge, followed by a pleasant walk through the trees. Go over a plank bridge then a larger bridge into the next meadow where the grass may be longer. The winding path continues to follow the river through a copse and onto a lane.

3 Turn left along the lane and pass over the road bridge. At the

road T-junction turn right and watch out for the next footpath, which is tucked away on the left on a straight stretch of the road. Follow this to where there is a path crossroads. Turn left, going down a pleasant tree-lined track. When you reach the cottages take the right fork to the main road.

4 Take the Bungay road opposite. Continue to a road

◆ Background Notes ◆

The **museum** is free to enter and children can be shown how to do brass rubbings. This is the art of rubbing wax crayons onto old brass memorials, which can be found in churches. They make a good picture to hang on the wall. The materials are provided by the museum. There is also a hands-on display of pottery and old fossils, including some dinosaur bones! The history of Halesworth throughout the ages is described and all about the 150-year-old railway station – with some model trains to be seen. Another display depicts the workshop of tailor Fred Knights of Halesworth, together with his sewing machine, bales of material, cottons, needles, thimbles, buttons and zips, all of which have been donated to the museum. Log on to www.halesworth.ws/museum for opening times or telephone 01986 873030.

The **railway** came to Halesworth in 1854 and this caused the decline of the river trade. In less than 30 years the last sailing wherry left the quay in Halesworth. Trading wherries could carry 25 tons of goods.

In case the children lost count – there are **10 bridges**, including the road bridge. And you pass through **7 gates**, including the one at the railway station.

Holton windmill

named Orchard Valley and turn left up this road. Then take the first turning on the right along a residential street. Turn left just before the end and then right at the T-junction and follow the footpath sign over a bridge and through a field by a wind turbine. When you reach the next path junction, go left up through the trees and when you emerge from the trees, go straight on. At the corner of the field go left then almost immediately right through a gap in the hedge past some swing tyres to a track.

5 Turn left down the track. Pass the cemetery. Just past Orchard House on the right, watch out for a narrow stony footpath. This bends left, passing the recreation ground, and takes you into a residential cul-de-sac. Proceed towards the roundabout but just before you get there you will see a gate to the railway station on the left. Cross the railway line carefully at the end of the platform and go out the other side to the car park.

Thorpeness

Pine Cones and Sea Shells

Thorpeness is a good venue for children of all ages. It has a beach and a boating lake and there is an interesting windmill, open to the public more frequently than any other windmill I know. Here is a pleasant walk in the surrounding countryside and all of the above are included. On the way round, you can see the House in the Clouds – the famous Thorpeness landmark.

Getting there *From the A12 between Woodbridge and Lowestoft, take the A1094 towards Aldeburgh. Take a left turn onto the B1069 and Thorpeness is at the end.*

Length of walk 2¾ miles.
Time 1½ hours.
Terrain There are no stiles to negotiate and a fairly flat terrain with good paths, making for easy walking.
Start/Parking The pay and display car park (all-day tickets available) opposite the boating lake (GR 472595).
Map OS Explorer 212 Woodbridge & Saxmundham.
Refreshments There is the Beach House, which is licensed and has

The Walk

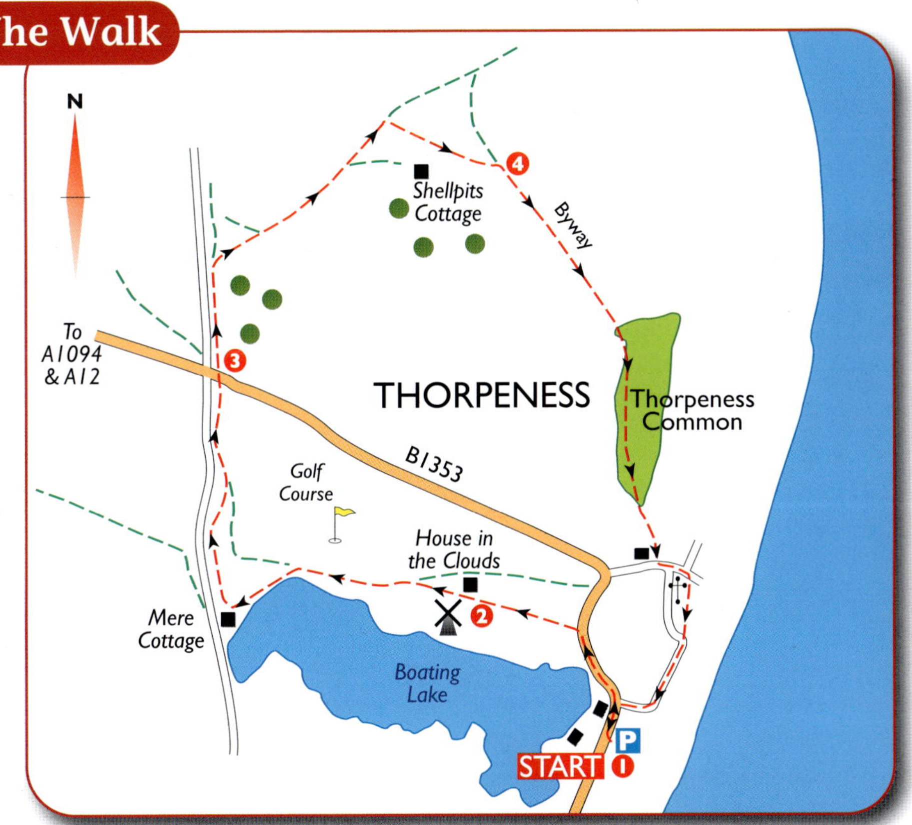

18

a play area for young children. The boating lake has a café and next to the almshouses further along in the village is the Dolphin pub, which has a large garden.

1 Turn right out of the car park and at the road junction, turn left towards Aldringham. Proceed along the road (called The Haven) and past the boating lake. Just after the turning to the Thorpeness Hotel and Golf Club, go left up the footpath (Uplands Road) signed to the windmill. Follow the wide dirt track and before long you will come across

the House in the Clouds on the right and, on the opposite side of the track, the windmill.

2 Continue to the tarmac road and take the footpath on the right of the track by the golf course, heading gently downhill. The path goes through the trees and then alongside the golf course with the river on the left. Then it continues through another wooded area and a vegetation of ferns. When you reach Mere Cottage, turn right in front of the cottage *before* the junction at the end, keeping the cottage on your left and going

◆ Fun Things to See and Do ◆

Visit Thorpeness Windmill (see 'Background Notes'), which is unusual in that it is open to the public much more frequently than most windmills. You can visit every day in the afternoon in July and August and at weekends it is open between April and mid September from 11 am to 1 pm and 2 pm to 5 pm. It is free to visit but donations for the upkeep of the windmill are always welcome.

On the shingle beach, the children can collect **pebbles and sea shells**. Many of the stones have interesting colours and shapes. There are cockle shells, mussels, whelks, oyster shells and lots of others.

It is fun for all the family to hire a rowing boat and **take a trip on the Boating Lake**, known as Thorpeness Meare.

along a leafy track. Then before you reach the stone track, take the turning to the right, marked by a wooden post with a black arrow and the sign of a bird. Follow the grass path and at the next post go straight on to a clearing by the barn and turn left along a wide dirt track, which becomes stony. This takes you to the road.

3 Go straight over along the byway opposite, a concrete track. This turns sharply to the right. After the private turning to Shellpits Cottage, you arrive at a junction by the Conservation Area gate. Here you turn right and follow the signed footpath through the woods. When you come to a clearing, bear left and continue through the woods. Children can collect pine cones here. The path comes to another junction by the RSPB information board, where you turn right.

4 The byway continues for some distance and eventually comes to another junction, where you turn right along a wide dirt track. Soon after, you turn off left along the byway on a wide grassy track.

The House in the Clouds, once a water tower

Almost ahead of you is the church and the House in the Clouds can be seen further to the right. When you reach the cottages go left and then immediately right, following the byway sign. The stony path takes you to the road. Continue up Church Road opposite, taking you to the seafront. The road bends right and right again to the junction by the boating lake. Turn left past the Beach House to bring you back to the car park.

18

◆ Background Notes ◆

The earliest windmills were **post mills**. Their name derives from the fact that the windmill was built around one large upright post of timber, which could pivot and so be turned, allowing the whole structure to face into the wind. The frame was built of wood so they were relatively easy and fast to build. They had to be manoeuvrable, yet sturdy enough to stand the test of time. The first mills were built with the central post, usually made of elm, resting on a cross-shaped oak base, but later the stability of the post mill was increased by building a round base of brick with a conical roof, which carried to the underside of the timber body of the windmill or buck. This roundhouse protected the cross frame from the weather and also provided the miller with useful storage space. It usually had two doors, one on each side, so that if the sails of the windmill obstructed the door on one side it was possible to use the other one. The main post passed up into the roof of the windmill, which at first was a normal pitched roof, but later it was found that the brake wheel had more room if the roof was given curved rafters and so many post mills have a familiar round shaped roof. Access to the windmill was by means of a wooden ladder or staircase.

Because the windmill was made of wood and fairly light in weight, it was actually possible to dismantle and move the whole windmill to another location, and **Thorpeness Windmill** is an example of this. It was originally built as a corn mill in the neighbouring village of Aldringham in 1803. But after it stopped working it was moved to Thorpeness and adapted to pump water to the nearby water tower, which is now the converted **House in the Clouds** on the opposite side of the footpath. This is now a holiday home available for rent.

This book contains other walks in Suffolk that have windmills en route or nearby. Holton (see Walk 17) has a post mill, and there are tower mills at Buxhall and Pakenham.

Walberswick

Crabbing Country

Walberswick is an old fishing village with a small community, over the other side of the River Blyth from the town of Southwold whose lighthouse and church are easily visible from the river's edge. This route includes the beautiful village, the surrounding heathland, which is an Area of Outstanding Natural Beauty, and a stretch alongside the Dunwich River, with the North Sea to the east. You have the option of shortening the circuit at point 3, if you wish. A pair of binoculars would be useful on the walk as there is plenty of wildlife to see.

19

Getting there *From the A12 between Lowestoft and Ipswich, turn off south of Blythburgh onto the B1387, which leads directly to Walberswick.*

Length of walk 1½ or 2½ miles.
Time ¾ hour or 1¼ hours.
Terrain There are some stiles to negotiate at the beginning but the paths are good and there is very little road walking.
Start/Parking In the paying car park at the end of the village in Ferry Road by the river (GR 500749).
Map OS Explorer 231 Southwold & Bungay.
Refreshments There is the Potters Wheel Tea Room on the village green near the end of the walk and not far from the car park is the Bell Inn, which has an extensive garden.

The Walk

1 Just before the entrance to the car park by the ticket booth, you will see a footpath on each side of the road. As you leave the car park take the one on the right to Old Vicarage Cottage. Go to the right side of the cottage grounds, over a bank, with the path then cutting through some grass to a stile by a ditch. Proceed across the field, keeping close to the ditch and reed beds on the left. At the next stile take the wide path to the left that goes uphill and through the trees to the lane.

2 Turn right. The lane bends to the left and you arrive at a road junction. Take the footpath directly opposite, going past a tennis court. Continue straight on at the path junction and walk down to where the path bends sharply right, then straight on again at the next junction. When you reach the next junction, with the bridleway, turn left. Go through the trees to the next path junction by the Walberswick Nature Reserve Information Board.

3 *For the short walk*, take the left path (which rejoins the route at point 5). *For the full walk*, go right. Proceed along by the field, then the path bends right, going uphill past a seat with a view and then a Second World War pillbox. At the T-junction, turn left and keep to the path on the right at the next junction. Soon you follow a

◆ Fun Things to See and Do ◆

Crabbing in the River Blyth by the harbour is great fun. Take a bucket and a piece of string with you. Attach some food, such as a small piece of bread or meat (a piece of bacon is a favourite), to the end of the string by means of a safety pin. Drop the end into the lake and lift out the crabs, which attach themselves to the string. If you keep the crabs in a bucket of water, don't forget to put them all back at the end. And wash your hands as soon as you can afterwards!

There are plenty of birds to spot on the river and if you have some binoculars with you, the landmarks at nearby Southwold can be seen, including the lighthouse.

meandering path through the trees, past a second pillbox and another seat. Then a wooden walkway is provided for the route through the reed beds to a fork in the footpath. Take the left path, which leads you up a bank where you turn left again and reach an old brick-built wind pump.

4 Here you turn left down the steps, over a wooden bridge and along another wooden walkway by the Dunwich River. Proceed straight on along the path which runs parallel with the river. After some distance you arrive at another fork, where you turn right. If you have taken the short route, you will also arrive at this junction where you now turn left.

5 Follow the path through the reed beds to the bridge on the right, which you cross, taking you to the beach. Turn left and you can choose to walk along the top on the beach path with sea views or, in cold weather, you can use the sheltered narrower path which runs parallel near the foot of the bank. Before the black beach huts, take the hard path on the left, bringing you back across the river by the bridge. Bear right up the track and turn right by the public toilets along the byway. Children like to walk along the sea wall. At the end, take the steps on the left and proceed along the sandy path by the river back to the car park where you started.

◆ Background Notes ◆

Walberswick is a pretty English village on the coast, which is very popular, especially in summer. The **parish church, St Andrew's**, which you pass as you enter the village, is over 500 years old and was once very large – evidence of the wealth of Walberswick – but had to be partly dismantled in the 1690s so that repairs and restoration could be made to the remaining building.

The **British Open Crabbing Championship** usually takes place in Walberswick at the beginning of August each year and has several hundred entries (a total of over 1,200 has been known!). It is not how many crabs you can catch, but who can attract the heaviest crab over the ninety minute period of the competition. The cost to enter is £1 and the winner receives £50 and a gold medal.

Carlton Colville

Wildlife on the Broad

Here is a walk on the shorter side, which begins in a quiet and remote area where there is some interesting wildlife, but you have the option and the opportunity to explore the nearby commercial and lively area of Oulton Broad, popular with the boating community. You can leave the route when you reach the marina and enter a park area with public access where you can browse around the various activities available, lots of which will appeal to children.

Getting there *Take the A146 Beccles to Lowestoft road and soon after the junction with the A1145 look out for the sign to the Wildlife Centre which is a turning on the left onto Burnt Hill Lane.*

Length of walk 2 miles.
Time 1 hour.
Terrain Fairly flat with mostly good paths although some narrow ones at the beginning.
Start/Parking In the free car park at the Carlton Marshes Education Centre at the end of Burnt Hill Lane (GR 508921).
Map OS Explorer OL40 Lowestoft.
Refreshments Ivy House Country Hotel en route, which has a lovely old barn converted to a tearoom.

1 From the car park, turn right down the lane and onto a bridleway to reach a metal gate and soon after go through a kissing gate on the right. This is a narrow grass path, which runs alongside a water channel. Pass

The Walk

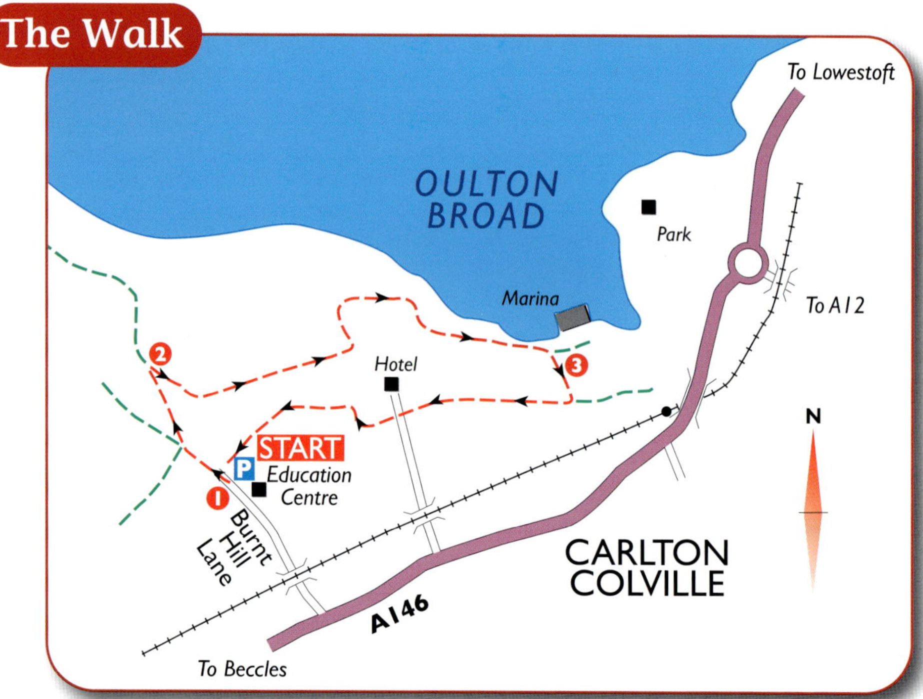

over two wooden railway sleeper bridges and continue to another kissing gate, which takes you over a ditch and up a bank onto a raised path. Turn right.

2 You start to head back towards the Centre but the path swings left with dykes on either side. At the path junction continue straight on and go over a stile, forcing you left towards Oulton Broad Water where you may spot the sails of the yachts.

The path turns right along a stony track, and then turns right and left again along a sheltered route through the trees. It emerges into the open with Oulton Broad Water on the left. Go through the gap in the fence to the marina. Here you can go straight on through the marina past the toilet block to the park (see 'Fun Things to See and Do') and return to this point later.

3 Otherwise, turn right along a

◆ Fun Things to See and Do ◆

At point 3 on the map, you may wish to visit the **Nicholas Everitt Park at Oulton Broad** where there are many activities. This would add another mile onto your journey there and back. There is crazy golf, a pets' corner (entrance fee to pay) and a children's play area. There is also a museum and the opportunity to take a boat trip on the broads – you can go on an organised trip or hire your own boat. There are also picnic areas and places for ice cream and refreshment. More details from the website www.visit-oultonbroad.co.uk or telephone Lowestoft Tourist Information: 01502 533600.

During the walk, especially the first stages around the nature reserve, the children can try to identify the many **water creatures** found in the dykes. They can also see how many different species of **dragonfly** they can spot in summer – these have amazing iridescent colours and can be seen hovering over the water and the reed beds with their two sets of wings. The dykes have **plants** with wonderful names such as lesser spearwort, water soldier and bogbean!

wide path and when you reach the caravans by the pink gate, turn right along the footpath, part of the Angles Way. The path then emerges into a meadow of wild flowers in season and trees. Go over a stile into the next meadow and then over another stile to the access road to the Ivy House Country Hotel where you may wish to stop for a break. Take the stile on the other side of the access track into a horse field. At the next stile you are forced right, then the path turns left. Go straight on at the path junction along by a deep water channel. This soon brings you directly back to the car park by the visitor centre.

◆ Background Notes ◆

The **Norfolk Broads** is an area of rivers and lakes (known as broads); it has the same status as a National Park and since 1989 has been managed by the Broads Authority. But the name is a slight misnomer because 'the Broads' also includes some of Suffolk, with **Oulton Broad** being the most southerly of the broads. Many are open to navigation and so the area is popular with all sorts of sailing and motor craft, which can be seen on this walk. The broads were thought to be natural but in fact they were formed from large pits dug by the Church during medieval times so that peat could be sold to the local towns and cities, particularly Norwich. When the sea level rose, the pits flooded and formed the landscape we see today.

The **Carlton Marshes Education Centre**, where the walk starts, aims to educate young children about wildlife issues and to preserve and conserve the habitat found nearby, whilst allowing the public to enjoy the reserve. Comprising grazing marsh, fens and peat pools, the reserve is drained by a system of man-made dykes – water channels that run all around the site and create a paradise for wading birds and water wildlife. The special creatures to be found here are water voles, freshwater snails, and no fewer than 15 species of dragonfly have been spotted. Barn owls, various warblers, marsh harriers and kestrels live on the reserve. The Centre runs special children's activities during the holidays, including sessions on wildlife art, photography, water creatures and much more. Telephone: 01502 564250.